Palgrave Studies of Internationalization in Emerging Markets

Emerging market nations such as Russia, Brazil, China, South Africa and India as well as Eastern European territories, are in the process of changes and growth that require specific study and attention. The international business strategies employed in these territories target new opportunities, the study of which provides scholars the opportunity to evolve international business theory.

Covering three main themes - international business, management and marketing –**Palgrave Studies of Internationalization in Emerging Markets** will encompass a multiplicity of topics. Examining the new ways in which firms from emerging economies develop and implement their internationalization strategy, as well as their management and marketing strategies, the series will encompass specific issues such as social entrepreneurship, operations and regional specifics of internationalization. Looking closer at the specifics underlying the development of emerging market nations and their firms, this series aims to shed light on the current and future issues associated with the challenges and opportunities offered by the varying contexts of emerging markets.

The book proposals for this series undergo a single blind peer review by three specialized highly respected established academics out of a pool of 28. The book proposal is sent to the reviewers that are selected based on its specific topic and content taking into consideration the geographic contextual specificity. The reviews with specific comments and recommendations are sent to the authors/editors of the perspectives publication who address them. Afterwards, the revised book proposal is evaluated by the Commissioning Editor of Palgrave Macmillan and Book Series Editor. The final manuscript is single blind peer reviewed. For more information on our peer review policy please see our website: https://www.palgrave.com/gp/book-authors/your-career/early-career-researcher-hub/peer-review-process?countryChanged=true

For information on how to submit a book proposal for inclusion in this series please contact Liz Barlow: liz.barlow@palgrave.com. For details on the book proposal process please visit our website: https://www.palgrave.com/gp/book-authors/publishing-guidelines/submit-a-proposal

More information about this series at
http://www.palgrave.com/gp/series/15456

Francesca Spigarelli • John R. McIntyre
Editors

The New Chinese Dream

Industrial Transition in the Post-Pandemic Era

palgrave
macmillan

Editors
Francesca Spigarelli
Department of Law
University of Macerata
Macerata, Macerata, Italy

John R. McIntyre
Georgia Tech CIBER
Scheller College of Business
Atlanta, GA, USA

ISSN 2662-1185 ISSN 2662-1193 (electronic)
Palgrave Studies of Internationalization in Emerging Markets
ISBN 978-3-030-69811-9 ISBN 978-3-030-69812-6 (eBook)
https://doi.org/10.1007/978-3-030-69812-6

This Palgrave Macmillan imprint is published by the registered company Springer Nature Switzerland AG.
The registered company address is: Gewerbestrasse 11, 6330 Cham, Switzerland

Preface

As we go to press with this volume, let me unabashedly paraphrase Winston Churchill: "it is, perhaps, the end of the beginning" of the Covid-19 pandemic. China is the largest country to have successfully managed its outbreaks and is maintaining strict border controls and immediate overwhelming response to prevent new infection clusters from getting out of hand. These measures plus the rollout of effective vaccines will, by the time this volume is published, bring us to the beginning of the end. At that point, a weary and wary world will look at China's governance model of central control that builds on a selective narrative, which the chapters in this volume so ably explore, and decide how to respond to the China alternative to sorely-tested post-war liberal democratic institutions of governance.

The Chinese government, under the Party's direction, announced the eradication of extreme poverty last December, it is in the process of devising its fourteenth five-year plan and its vision for 2035 (advancing one of the centenary goals to be reasonably sure that Mr. Xi will be able to enjoy meeting it in person) and is determined to achieve global pre-eminence in a variety of sectors. A concerted effort also is being made to address inequities and other imbalances arisen from the past forty years of growth and development. Success, or the perception thereof, in addressing these fundamental issues in a more balanced way will allow the Chinese Communist Party to ensure its continuing grip on power.

Covid-19 presented a crisis and an opportunity. China's government has so far been able to draw on the advantages of being a mobilization state to maximize the opportunity. But the shape of post-crisis China, indeed of the globe, is not yet clear. The Chinese Globalization Association has supported research and publication work focused on China's engagement with the world and its many implications for almost fifteen years. This volume is a result of scientific discussions preparing for, and benefiting from, the CGA's annual China Goes Global conference held on-line in 2020. It presents needed explorations of trends in the life sciences, aviation, advanced technology, innovation policy, diplomacy and other areas that were underway before the pandemic, and analyses how they will emerge when we are, finally, at the end of this crisis, and beyond.

Cambridge, MA Julian Chang
January 2021

Contents

Notes on Contributors

Nuoya Chen has served as a Marie Curie Fellow for the Health related Activity Recognition System based on IoT project at University of Macerata.

Her research focuses on business model and marketing strategy innovation for the use of AI and IoT in the healthcare sector. She worked at Philips Research (Eindhoven), Philips Research, University of China Academy of Science, Fudan University, Bremen University and KU Leuven. Nuoya attended the World Bank Youth Summit on Smart Cities and lead a team for the case challenge on using IoT for national healthcare emergencies, presented at Innovation for Healthcare Moonshot Session, International digital health-tech, healthcare & pharmacy conference.

Before joining University of Macerata, Ms. Chen studied and worked in Berlin, Johannesburg and Paris, Stockholm and London.

Marco R. Di Tommaso is Full Professor of Applied Economic Studies at the Department of Civil, Chemical, Environmental, and Materials Engineering, University of Bologna. He has studied in Italy and the UK. He has been visiting professor in China and in the USA. He has actively participated in the debate within the scientific community by presenting his works at seminars, workshops and conferences both in Italy and abroad. His books and papers have been published and diffused at the national and international level. He has collaborated with Italian and foreign universities, specialized research centres, international institutions (UNIDO, CEPAL, UNDP, OECD) and national and local governments.

His research focuses on the following topics: industrial sectors; industrial policy; local development, SMEs and clusters; international industry; Chinese economy and industry; health industry.

Fabio dos Santos Cardoso (M.Sc., Business Analyst) is Ph.D. Candidate in Business Management in the School of Economics and Management at the University of Minho. He is also senior business analyst in the Brazilian National Statistics Office (IBGE). He has extensive experience in digital transformation, business processes management, and international business. His main research areas are: Technology Adoption, Organizational Network, and International Business. He is a member of the Data Science Portugal, and StackOverFlow communities.

Peter Enderwick is an economist specialising in the field of international business. He is currently Professor of International Business at AUT University in Auckland New Zealand. Between 1988 and 2004 he was Professor of International Management at the University of Waikato. He has held visiting positions at the Helsinki School of Economics and Business, Finland; the University of South Australia, Adelaide; Thammasat Business School Bangkok; and the Centre for International Business University of Leeds UK. He is the author of nine books and has published more than 100 journal articles and book chapters. His research interests are in globalisation and labour, large emerging markets such as China and India and global factory systems. He is a member of the Academy of International Business and a founding member of ANZIBA (Australia-New Zealand International Business Academy).

Risto Herrala (phd) is adviser at the Bank of Finland research institute for emerging market studies (BOFIT). He has worked as senior economist at the International Monetary Fund (IMF) and the European Central Bank (ECB). He has extensive experience of analysis of emerging market and central banking issues. His research fields include emerging markets, the global economy, and macro-finance.

James R. Hoadley has worked as Associate Director of the Georgia Tech CIBER since 2005. He lived in Japan for nearly eight years, where he worked for Seiko Epson Corporation. He also worked as Human Resources manager for a Japanese-owned auto parts supplier in South Carolina before coming to Georgia Tech. He has an MBA from Georgia Tech and a graduate diploma in foreign language teaching and B.A. in international studies from the University of South Carolina. He has conducted doctoral studies at the Grenoble Ecole de Management in France. He has been co-author on peer-reviewed journal articles and book chapters on a variety of topics including Japanese foreign direct investment and Chinese industrial policy.

Dominique Jolly is Professor of Business Strategy at Webster University Geneva (Switzerland)where he chairs the Walker School of Business & Technology. He previously worked for SKEMA Business School (Sophia-Antipolis, France), the Center on China Innovation at CEIBS (Shanghai, China), HEC Montréal (Montréal, Canada) and Grenoble Ecole de Management (Grenoble, France). He works as a consultant for several large companies. He also advises international organizations and foreign governments in the areas of innovation and technology. His assignments have taken him to over twenty countries in Europe, Asia, North America, South America and Africa.

Dominique Lepore has a post doc position at the Department of Law (University of Macerata). She holds an Industrial Ph.D. in Global Studies (University of Macerata). She holds a Master's Degree in International Economics and Commerce. Her research activities are mainly related to Industry 4.0 national plans, Smart Specialization Strategies, Digital Innovation Hubs and technological innovation in China. She is a member of the c.MET05 National Centre for Applied Economic Studies. She also collaborates as an instructional designer and lecturer in ISTAO, Business School located in Ancona (Italy). She has participated in research projects, conferences and teaching activities in Italy, China, Croatia, Ethiopia, Poland and Spain.

Olena Liakh is an industrial PhD candidate in legal sciences at the University of Macerata, with a background in international business and commerce. She is currently carrying out applied research that helps to connect corporate practices with contributions towards a more global sustainable development. Her research interests include the analysis of global industrial policies and cost-benefit evaluations of healthcare systems, as well as more business-related topics, such as corporate responsibility and sustainability, integrated sustainability-controlling systems (particularly with regards to SMEs and business groups), sustainability evaluation systems, sustainable global value chains, green management, and sustainability leadership and culture.

Yin Li is Assistant Professor of Public Policy at the School of International Relations and Public Affairs, Fudan University. He holds a PhD in Public Policy from Georgia Institute of Technology, a Master in Regional Economics from University of Massachusetts Lowell, and a bachelor's degree in economics from Renmin University of China. His research interest includes science and technology policy, economics of innovation and development, and emerging technology governance, with a focus on China. His research was published in innovation study journals, including *Research Policy*, *Technovation*, and *The Journal of Technology Transfer*.

John R. McIntyre is founding Executive Director of the Georgia Tech CIBER, a national center of excellence, professor of management (Strategy and Innovation Area) in the Scheller College of Business He received his graduate education at Northeastern University, Strasbourg University, McGill University, completing his Ph.D. at the University of Georgia. Prior to joining Georgia Tech in September 1981, he was Research Associate for International Management at the Dean Rusk Center of the University of Georgia Law School. He has published in journals such as Technology and Society, Public Administration Quarterly, International Management Review, Defence Analysis, Studies in Comparative and International Development, The Journal of European Marketing, Politique Internationale, International Executive, International Trade Journal, among others. Author or coauthor thirteen book and over 120 trade and journal articles. He is the recipient of the State of Georgia Governor's International Award for international business education in 2009; the French National Order of Merit (Knight), 2009; the Georgia Tech-wide Steven Denning Faculty Award for Global Engagement, 2015; he was made honorary professor at ICN Graduate School of Business, University of Lorraine, France, 2017. He has been a consultant to numerous private and public sector organizations.

Maria Papageorgiou is a PhD Candidate of International relations at the University of Minho, Portugal, and Integrated Member of the Research Centre for Political Science (CICP). Currently she is a Visiting Researcher in the School of Geography, Politics and Sociology at Newcastle University and a Mentor at the New Silk Roads Academy based at International Institute for Asian studies, Leiden University. She holds a Master of Arts in International Political Economy from Panteio University, Greece and a Bachelor's degree in International and European studies from Piraeus University, Greece. She has also been visiting researcher at ICD in Berlin, Germany and University of Maribor, Slovenia. Her main research interests are great powers relations with a focus on alignment and cooperation, international political economy, military studies and social media as a tool of foreign policy.

Gianluca Sampaolo is pursuing an industrial doctorate in the field of Blue Economy at the University of Macerata. Sinologist, he graduated with honors in Global Politics and International Relations. During both his undergraduate and graduate years, he has accumulated various international study and work experiences, mainly in China and the U.S. He has been part of the scientific debate by means of disseminating his contributions at both national and international conferences. Since 2019, he has been responsible for the "Economics of China" class at the Confucius Institute of the University of Macerata. His research interests primarily focus on the evaluation of global industrial policies for Blue Economy but also range from international business, international relations, U.S.-China relations, geopolitics, politics and economics of China.

Francesca Spigarelli (prof., dr.) is full professor of Applied Economics, at the University of Macerata and Director of the China Center. She is Vice Rector for Entrepreneurship and Technological Transfer and for European research policy.

She has extensive experience as coordinator of EU funded projects (7°PF and Horizon 2020).

Her main teaching areas are: International Business, Applied Economics, Microeconomics. Her research fields cover: Industrial policies, Chinese investments, internationalization processes of SMEs, Chinese economy.

She is member of the board of Chinese Globalization Association.

List of Figures

List of Charts

Introduction

"The New Chinese Dream: Industrial Transition in the Post-Pandemic Era" is a book centered on the idea that the massive use of selective industrial policies, systematically adjusted in case of internal crisis and external shocks, has been the driving force for a Chinese transition towards economic supremacy by year 2049, the centennial year of the Chinese state establishment.

Over the past forty years China has gone through a number of significant reforms, developing what has been officially referred to as a socialist market economy with unique Chinese characteristics. These reforms have stimulated a massive structural shift both of the economy and society leveraging on profound transformation of the Chinese national industrial system.

The Covid-19 pandemic outbreak happened at a crucial juncture for the country—in the middle of a new transition period towards the ambitious achievement of a "New Chinese dream" by 2049 and various intermediary time-bounded goals set over the recent past. China aims simultaneously to achieve the status of a fully developed country as well as that of global innovation leader. At the same time, it also seeks to resolve structural issues related to internal social and territorial imbalances and divides, environmental deterioration, uneven access to healthcare and social services.

At the beginning of 2020, the country was bridging several structural changes of its economy and society, pushed by key reforms described in Chap. 1 (Belt and Road Initiative, to Made in China 2025), and engage in a sustained globalization-driven thrust reflected in the ongoing trade war with the US. Such changes and related challenges have been, in some cases, "suspended" or, in other cases, altered by the global pandemic. As described in the first Chapter, while implementing prompt and short-term oriented interventions, targeting both the demand and the supply side of the economy, the government surfed the Pandemic wave to activate a new long-term planning exercise. Summer 2020 was dominated by the concept of the so-called "dual circulation—双循环 (shuāng xúnhuán)" strategy (hereinafter "DCS") promoting a further round of industrial and economic policies trying to secure the achievement of the 2049 goal.

The book is articulated on a careful and reviewed selection of papers from the 14th China Goes Global Conference (2020). It describes and explains structural changes that China is experiencing in the economy at large (as reflected in Chaps. 1 and 2) and in strategic industries (as in Chaps. 3, 4, 5, 6, 7, and 8), in the light of 2049 goals set by the Chinese government to turn the country into a fully advanced and developed nation. The likelihood of China achieving a the leading position in both process and state of the art innovation is considered, particularly in the wake of the ongoing global pandemic and the manner in which it was addressed.

Specifically, Chap. 2 analyzes select macro-economic data to show how Chinese export growth has slowed down dramatically over the past ten years. While the slowdown in part reflects a shift in Chinese economic policies, it has also been accompanied by significant international tensions. Chinese influence is increasingly resisted around the world, as indicated by the broadsides of trade wars and select protectionist measures faced by Chinese firms and products abroad. The chapter reviews the underlying tensions between China and its export partners and projects the Chinese path in the global economy.

Chapter 3 considers Chinese growing innovative capacity and inputs to science and technology leading to "state of the art" innovation. To date, technology catch-up by emerging economies such as China has been largely sequential, imitative, and reached through established networks. However, attempts to achieve frontier technologies such as Industry 4.0 present significant new challenges impacting knowledge sources, knowledge types, and transfer processes. The chapter argues that to achieve innovation leadership, Chinese firms need to vary and widen their knowledge sources, to develop both predictive capabilities (in evaluating new technologies), and combinative capabilities (integrating them with the necessary skills and resources). Despite the deteriorating international business environment that China is currently facing, China would appear the best placed of all the major emerging economies to achieve this transformation.

Chapter 4 sheds light on how China is leveraging both its diplomacy and its extensive network of strategic partnerships in power projection to achieve the 2049 centennial goals. The authors investigate the role of China's strategic partnerships in its global rise by borrowing elements of the network model from business studies and by drawing on similarities in a firm's internationalization process. By focusing on three overlapping dimensions—economic, military, and political—the authors show that China has developed a global network of interconnectivity to uphold and further develop its economic capacity, secure a stable geopolitical environment across its borders, modernize its army, alleviate US pressure in South East Asia, and eventually facilitate its global rise.

The remaining chapters of the book highlight specific sectoral patterns in the Chinese industrial economy which play a strategic role in 2049 centennial ambitions: ICT and advanced technology, life science, aerospace, semiconductor.

Chapter 5 addresses the digital landscape in China. The author argues that China has succeeded over the past twenty years in articulating and implementing a strategic vision of a powerful national system of innovation, and that this system has begun to yield significant technological results in the digital transformation fields. This contribution also lists various reasons as to the dramatic growth of digital fields inside China–including protectionism precluding US companies from penetrating the Chinese market, and the resulting preponderant influence of China due to its enormous population. Several examples of future possible application domains, such as driverless cars and smart cities, are considered. It must be recognized that China has been able to run its own digital world, responding to its innovatory and entrepreneurial growth needs. Several important impediments to the development of Chinese digital potential externally are discussed in the final section.

Chapter 6 investigates new trends in the life science sector, another leading edge industry, considering its impact on the long-term sustainability of the "New Chinese Dream". The authors discuss how the Chinese government is promoting innovation and competitiveness for the life-science sector, both to satisfy internal demand and to compete at the international level. Technological progress is the synergetic result of government interventions, aligning interests and efforts of academia, private business and public firms. Based also on recent achievements and on impact of measures in contrasting the spread of the Pandemic, the life-science sector in China bears the potential to become a world leading industry.

In Chapter 7, the authors consider the Chinese commercial aircraft manufacturing sector as one of the command heights of a global leading manufacturing economy. They review the technological and policy pathways in manufacturing world-class commercial aircraft. They conclude that China seems poised to repeat in aviation what it has done in train travel—to become the world's largest market. The original projections were for that to occur by 2024. COVID-19 has altered this pace. Unlike China's achievements in its extensive high-speed rail network, China is facing the realization that its civilian skies are filled with commercial planes made in places like Toulouse, France or Everett, Washington. The national government wants Chinese-made planes serving Chinese passengers on its air routes in China. This is in line with China's industrial upgrading, economic transformation, globalization, and rise as a global geopolitical power, as analyzed in Chaps. 1 and 2.

Chapter 8 goes deep into the analysis of another strategic sector: semiconductor. Restricting China's access to advanced semiconductor technology has become the U.S. government's chokepoint strategy in the emerging hi-tech cold war. The development of an indigenous semiconductor supply chain is increasingly vital for China's next stage of development. In this chapter, the author documents China's experience of semiconductor industry policy and development, and evaluate key Chinese players in the IC supply chain and their technological capabilities. A strategic look at the supply chain shows that China's semiconductor industry is resilient even under U.S. pressure, though significant weaknesses remain.

Chapter 9, the concluding chapter, provides historical and analytical perspectives on China's strengths and weaknesses in achieving the centennial goals which have driven the long path of Chinese economic history since its opening to the world economy. The chapter raises the fundamental question: have industrial policies worked? It reviews the question against the background of a fierce academic debate "over whether China should continue to exercise the industrial policies that undergirded its rise to prominence," as quoted scholars have noted. The chapter concludes on the emergence of a Chinese "third revolution" as a unique and differentiated policy model.

John R. McIntyre
Francesca Spigarelli

CHAPTER 1

Structural Changes and Policies in China: From the New Dream to COVID-19 Era

Gianluca Sampaolo, Marco R. Di Tommaso, and Olena Liakh

Abstract The work sheds light on the significant reforms that China has undertaken over the past 40 years and which, starting from the 1978 'Open Door Policy', stimulated a massive structural shift of the Chinese economy and society. The twenty first century pandemic happened at a linchpin moment for China, when the country was bridging several contentious structural changes due to the 'New Normal' paradigm and the more recent trade war with the US. In response to the Covid-19 outbreak and in the light of the upcoming release of the new 5-year plan, Chinese authorities promptly adopted a series of coordinated measures to support

G. Sampaolo (✉) • O. Liakh
Department of Law, University of Macerata, Macerata, Italy
e-mail: gianluca.sampaolo@unimc.it

M. R. Di Tommaso
Department of Civil, Chemical, Environmental and Material Engineering, University of Bologna, Bologna, Italy
e-mail: marco.ditommaso3@unibo.it

F. Spigarelli, J. R. McIntyre (eds.), *The New Chinese Dream*, Palgrave Studies of Internationalization in Emerging Markets,
https://doi.org/10.1007/978-3-030-69812-6_1

the national economy and engaged in a new long-term planning, the so-called "Dual Circulation Strategy". From the New Dream to the Covid-19 era, innovation and industrial policies are presented through the lens of political economy.

Keywords Structural changes • Industrial policy • Open Door • New Normal

1.1 Pre-COVID-19 Industrial Policies Shaping China's Innovation Potential

Over the past 40 years, China has gone through a number of significant reforms. Such careful planning and policies stimulated a massive structural shift, which had a drastic impact on society and economic growth, while profoundly transforming the country's industry. China is now among the world leaders in international rankings on GDP, export capacity, inward and outward foreign direct investments, and it has also improved many social development indicators, including quality of life and population access to education and health services.

As literature has already demonstrated (see Chap. 2), the Chinese government introduced several structural reform policies under the guidance of Deng Xiaoping (Garnaut et al. 2018), starting in 1978. The Open Door Policy marked the first stage of a progressive industrial, institutional and social transition of China (Spigarelli 2018), from a planned economy to a "socialism with Chinese characteristics" (Choi 2011; Deng 1985; Dirlik 1989 and others). The intent was to rapidly "industrialize" the country by drawing on the technology, know-how and resources of Western companies, in exchange for low-cost labor and fiscal advantages. The combined effect of policies, growth of internal entrepreneurship and crucial sectors (stimulated through selective industrial policies), and the tying of economic growth to the "great international circulation", helped China conquer the status of "Factory of the World", first, and later that of the second most powerful world economy (Barbieri et al. 2010, 2015, 2017; Di Tommaso et al. 2013, 2019; Di Tommaso and Tassinari 2014). The country launched an additional strategy in 2000, known as Go Global, with the initial aim of gaining access to critical natural resources globally

(Alon et al. 2011). However, thanks to progressive waves of Chinese foreign direct investments in the global markets (Buckley et al. 2007; Deng 2009; Kolstad and Wiig 2012), this strategy turned out to have even more complex "returns" in international expansion, and securing access to foreign technology, knowledge and brands (Bellabona and Spigarelli 2007).

In this context of continuous structural change, however, the new Chinese globalized industrial system has also exacerbated socio-territorial imbalances and divides, and brought along the unprecedent challenge of environmental deterioration. What is more, the global financial crisis of 2008–2009 strongly affected international demand, forcing China to protect itself through an economic stimulus of 4 trillion Rmb. This stimulated growth to a certain extent but, at the same time, resulted in a massive debt and exceeded production capacity. In response to the crisis and the above challenges, the presidency of Xi Jinping designed the "New Normal" strategy,[1] as part of a set of new reforms. This plan prioritized sustainable growth, to be achieved through environmental protection, social wellbeing and healthcare equality. But it also focused on supporting the development of national industries, making China less dependent on foreign partners, as well as driving the country's innovation acceleration through domestic champion firms and more high-profile jobs (Barbieri et al. 2020; Ling and Quan 2017).

The "New Normal" strategy was deployed in correspondence with "two centenary goals" of the new "Chinese Dream", which were set to be achieved nationally, locally and at industrial level by 2021 and 2049 respectively (Ling and Quan 2017; Meidan et al. 2015; Saggu and Anukoonwattaka 2015): Chinese society should reach a moderate prosperity and become an innovative nation by 2021,[2] and it should achieve the status of fully developed country, as well as world innovation leader, by 2049.[3] Innovation became the key priority driver in the transition towards modernization and the Chinese government began "communicating" it in its official narrative (Di Tommaso et al. 2020a; Green and Stern 2015).

[1] In detail, the "New Normal" sanctions the new Chinese development model promoted for the first time by President Xi Jinping in May 2014. The "New Normal" embodies a focus on structural changes in the Chinese economic system and describes a growth model still marked but lower (around 7% per year over the next five years) and focused on quality (compared to quantity), both in terms of social distribution and environmental impact.

[2] One hundred years from the Communist Party of China's birth.

[3] One hundred years from the People's Republic of China's foundation.

In order to achieve those goals, a series of secondary, mid-term targets were set through the 13th five-year plan (2016–2020). They included, among others, the strive towards economic growth stability, improved environmental quality and healthier living conditions (CCCPC 2016).

Two additional strategies complemented the "New Normal" in supporting China's recognition as a key player in global value chains.

The first strategy was the Belt and Road initiative (BRI) (Huang 2016; Ferdinand 2016; Liu and Dunford 2016; Yu 2017; Chaisse and Matsushita 2018; Zhang et al. 2018; Liu and Zhang 2019). Formally announced by Xi Jinping in 2013, BRI was intended to strengthen bilateral economic, cultural, scientific and political ties between China and the territories located on the historic Silk and Maritime roads. Besides geo-political implications, BRI also aimed to support the transformation of the Chinese industrial system. In the circumstances of declining productivity, increasing labor expenses, and stricter environmental regulations, it was necessary for China to offshore excess capacity from the most labor-intensive and polluting industrial processes. This was accomplished through international cooperation in the forms of investment and bilateral trade agreements, Special Economic Zones, and better logistic infrastructures (Misiągiewicz and Misiągiewicz 2017; Spigarelli and Ping 2018; Fasulo 2019; Chang 2019).

The second policy, launched in 2015, was introduced in support of the Chinese global ambitions with specific regard to innovation supremacy: Made in China 2025 (MIC25) (Wübbeke et al. 2016; Hammer 2017; EUCCC 2017; Müller and Voigt 2018; Li 2018; Xu et al. 2018; Perskaya 2019). MIC25 is a comprehensive strategy and part of a wider 3-step plan. Its main objective is to expand Chinese innovative and technological capacity, from that of a low-end manufacturing country to that of a leading goods and services producer. In order to achieve this, the country is seeking to embed ICT within the manufacturing industry, as well as to reinforce basic materials, key components and existing technologies on the one hand, while also promoting its service-orientation on the other hand. In product terms, greater quality control is expected, together with the development and globalization of China's own brands. Thanks to the strengthening of green technologies, MIC25 should also promote progress towards environmental preservation. Selective industrial policies have been placing great emphasis on 10 core sectors, including advanced IT, high-speed rail transport and ultra-high voltage power equipment, in which China aspires to leapfrog Western economies, new materials, for which over 500 new industrial parks have been created, as well as medical devices, robotics, green energy, aerospace, shipping, and agricultural machinery (Chang 1994; Bianchi and Labory 2018; ISDP 2018; Petti et al. 2016; Rodrik 2008; Wübbeke et al. 2016; Zenglein and Holzmann 2019). In addition to policy actions, a set of guideline documents have been published to support the growth of each of the afore-mentioned priority sectors. Some examples include the "Guidelines for the Pharmaceutical Industry Development Plan" for healthcare (Zenglein and Holzmann 2019; Di Tommaso et al. 2020a) and Document 625 (2016) on renewable electricity purchase. Moreover, special attention has been given to solar/wind limitation reduction targets for firms and provinces (2018),[4] and to acceleration pilot projects for service robots and national robotics standards (around 60 were expected by 2020).[5]

Following MIC25, a second plan, spanning from 2026 to 2035, aspires to promote the buildout of an "average" Chinese innovation capacity within world manufacturing. And finally, during 2036–2049, the country will try to position itself as a world innovation leader (Petti et al. 2016; Wübbeke et al. 2016).

Considering all these industrial policies and trends, it can be easily foreseen how China's race towards innovation development and global expansion, driven by the potential of specific key sectors, may soon elevate the status of the country to that of a world innovation leader. This race to innovation leadership, however, has also been impacted by the COVID-19 pandemic.

1.2 New Scenarios and Old Challenges: China and the COVID-19 Outbreak

The pandemic outbreak happened at a crucial time for China. The country was bridging several structural changes, pushed by the reforms highlighted above, to its economy and society, and was at the same time engaged in globalization-driven issues. Such changes and related challenges have been, in some cases, temporarily "suspended" or, in other instances, altered by the pandemic.

[4] See: https://www.oxfordenergy.org/wpcms/wp-content/uploads/2020/06/Current-direction-for-renewable-energy-in-China.pdf.

[5] See: https://www.chinadaily.com.cn/china/2016-12/15/content_27672692.htm.

For a complete overview, it is important to begin with a discussion of China's new role in the global value chain, and the reshoring and relocation processes of production activities that were ongoing. At the end of 2019, the country was reshaping its manufacturing system (especially through the BRI) by offshoring excess capacity from domestic non-key industries towards less developed countries. In order to focus on high-tech global value chains, China has been transferring production capacity abroad, mainly among BRI countries. At the same time, certain areas of Southeast Asia promptly assumed a more central role as manufacturing powerhouses by offering low labor costs and good logistic positioning. Nevertheless, the outbreak of the pandemic impacted global value chains and the related concerns: with most economies in lockdown—partial or total—and with the contraction of global trade—estimated between 13% and 32% by the WTO—and of investments—estimated between 30% and 40% by UNCTAD—reshoring processes from China, and accelerated relocation and reshoring of many manufacturing facilities to Western countries and other locations in Asia began to take place (WTO 2020; UNCTAD 2020).

A second important aspect to consider is related to the trade war with the US and, more generally, the impact of the Trump Administration policies on global industry and trade (Li et al. 2018; Liu and Woo 2018; Chong and Li 2019; Wei 2019; Layne 2020; Di Tommaso et al. 2020b). The COVID-19 pandemic occurred in the middle of the trade war escalation with the US, driven by accusations of unfair commercial practices. Beginning in March 2018, a series of tariffs were levied by the Trump Administration, which had significant negative effects on the Chinese economy (see Chap. 2). It was the race for innovation supremacy that fueled the trade war, despite the complementarity of the two countries[6] in many industries. Beijing's efforts are becoming even more compelling, as the US tries to contain the rise of its geopolitical rival. The US has pressured allies to shun equipment from Huawei Technologies Co., barred dozens of China's largest tech companies from buying American parts, and even slapped bans on ByteDance Ltd.'s TikTok and Tencent Holdings Ltd.'s WeChat.

The pandemic has boosted certain internal processes (e.g. ICT, health innovation and investment) and exacerbated the war with the US, leading to a fourfold implication. First, the cross-country production (for

[6] The US exports drug formulations, China exports bulk drugs.

example, in the case of medical devices) between China and the US implies the overlay of a multiple tariff along the supply chain, resulting in a higher price of the final product (GlobalData Healthcare 2019). In the specific case of healthcare, where 25% tariffs on high-end medical devices were imposed, this could have repercussions on care accessibility of the lower-income population.[7] Second, FDI flows have begun to slow down, as American manufacturers are leaving the Chinese market, and some Chinese investments are being excluded from the US market (Newmarker 2019). Third, since Chinese students in the future might be restricted from accessing US universities, this could, among other impacts, erode the collaborative nature of scientific research. Finally, in the absence of cooperation between the US and China, other emerging countries (e.g. India) could step up and form new strategic alliances with them. Sensing these trends, China has already added new incentives for foreign investors through the 2019 Foreign Investment National Encouraged Catalogue (Hanemann et al. 2019; Rees 2019);

The rush to innovation was, in turn, altered and accelerated by the pandemic. Innovation in China is strictly linked to its digital ecosystem. The country's internet infrastructure, offering a three-tier service delivery, from fixed-line, mobile and education, is only one part of such an ecosystem, which was also profoundly defined by the activity of China's tech champions, known as BAT (Baidu, Alibaba, Tencent). The nation has built a unique digital context, based on the concept of autarchy and self-determination, in terms of technology, software solutions, social media and related services. The accumulated knowhow, along with the increasing development of Chinese technologies in data collection, processing, and machine learning, have greatly benefited some specific industries.

During the pandemic, China has demonstrated to the world its level of digitalization and innovation reached so far: from healthcare, robotics,[8] electric vehicles,[9] IoT and data monitoring. Indeed, the pandemic forced the country to switch its innovation focus from long-term objectives to short-term and COVID-19-related solutions. This, nevertheless,

[7] See: https://www.thelancet.com/journals/lancet/article/PIIS0140-6736(19)31908-7/fulltext.

[8] With industrial and service (+30% growth) robotics representing 36% of global installations and 2% of the Chinese market respectively (2019).

[9] China ranked 9th Below: $438.1 million (1.7%) compared with leader US ($7.9 billion, 30.5%) and Japan in 10th position ($431.5 million, 1.7%). See: http://www.worldstopexports.com/electric-cars-exports-by-country.

contributed to some unforeseen outcomes: the broadening of R&D's scope in key sectors, as well as the overcoming of previously existing legal barriers, allowed for some unexpected product uses. One such example is self-driving delivery vehicles, which were used by hospitals in order to provide patients and medical staff with meals, medical supplies and similar.[10] The massive use of artificial intelligence (AI) was also impressive. AI was applied during the emergency for remote patient management (Lv et al. 2019; Hsu et al. 2016; Li et al. 2014), medical diagnosis assistance (Wong 2019), and monitoring of people's health through wearable devices (Poon et al. 2011; Majumder et al. 2017).

Thanks to technology China has managed to bring the "3 T method" (test, track, treat) of combatting the pandemic to quite a high level. The measures adopted to keep the virus at bay seem to have paid off, shifting from containment to recovery, and ultimately guaranteeing reopening to the country and its economic ecosystem.

The Chinese economy is already showing signs of recovery in the second half of 2020, while the second wave of the pandemic seems to be under control, and without major impacts on the Chinese population.[11] The latest World Bank and IMF economic forecasts indicate 7.9%–8.2% growth rates for 2021, in stark contrast to the estimates of industrialized economies (World Bank 2020a, b; IMF 2020a). Similar positive trends are projected for the period 2022–2025. Although a slight decrease to 5.8% is expected in 2022, China's real GDP growth should settle towards 5.5% by 2025 (IFM 2020b).[12]

1.3 Post-COVID-19 Policies: The Dual Circulation Strategy

The reaction capacity and resilience shown by China during the pandemic (Gong et al. 2020) represent unique and intrinsic values that are common to other historical periods in Chinese history.[13] Initially criticized and

[10] See: https://www.unido.org/stories/china-robot-delivery-vehicles-deployed-help-covid-19-emergency.

[11] Based on last available data, the GDP growth in China was +3.2% in the second quarter (https://www.ft.com/content/4a0f9dca-b48c-453f-bfc1-2c6c8b55682a) and +4.9% in the third quarter (https://www.ft.com/content/22108ddd-3280-4013-bcd8-1adc9e6ae13d).

[12] As for October 2020.

[13] China has historically shown its resilience in difficult times and its capacity to react and re-start. Very well-known examples are the opium wars, the massacre of Nanking and the civil war from which the PRC was born.

affected by a hostility sentiment, especially from the West, China's example demonstrates that, with the right policies in place, there is light at the end of the tunnel. Macroeconomic policies can mitigate the economic costs associated with containment measures and support recovery, but timing is key and early intervention is paramount.

In fact, in response to the COVID-19 outbreak, Chinese Authorities promptly adopted a series of coordinated measures, supporting both the Chinese and foreign companies based in China, that ultimately helped mitigate the negative economic impact, especially on the most vulnerable (Reuters 2020; Xinhuanet 2020a, b; Zhang 2020). At the same time, long-term policies have been adjusted and reinforced. Measures that were taken by the government range from financial, fiscal, monetary, to administrative support.[14] The People's Bank of China set lending facilities with a capacity of more than 2 trillion RMB to fund loans for small businesses, poverty alleviation, and agricultural firms. Also, China's regulators encouraged the forbearance of small business loans. Fiscal policy measures and monetary policy, with easy access to loans, have been used as tools to support households and private firms' activities. The government is also leveraging on the role of SOEs to promote employment, push investments, and assist small and medium companies (Okamoto 2020). Other measures concern customs, promotion of e-commerce, facilitation for social security contributions and labor.[15] Also, through the economic stimulus approved at the end of May 2020, great attention was paid to advanced technology, promoting the so-called "new infrastructures"—high-speed railways, 5G, Big Data, AI, and columns for electric vehicles—[16] for a value that, in 2020, could exceed 2000 billion RMB (Fasulo 2020; Meinhardt 2020; Bloomberg 2020). All these measures reinforce the idea that China is eager to assert itself not only as a sales market but also as a manufacturing one from which to export.

[14] For a comprehensive list of monetary and fiscal policy measures adopoted by China to contrast the Pandemic, please refer to https://home.kpmg/xx/en/home/insights/2020/04/china-government-and-institution-measures-in-response-to-covid.html.

[15] Further information on the Covid-19 official policies can be found at: https://www.europeanchamber.com.cn/en/national-news/3125;

[16] See http://www.xinhuanet.com/english/2020-03/05/c_138846271.htm?from=singlemessage%2310006-weixin-1-52626-6b3bffd01fdde4900130bc5a2751b6d1 for more information about the "new infrastructure".

Despite the need for prompt and short-term oriented interventions, the government surfed the time of the Pandemic to activate a new long-term planning exercise, also in the light of the upcoming release of the new 5-year plan. In the ever-fruitful world of Chinese political dialectic, summer 2020 was dominated by the concept of the so-called "dual circulation—双循环 (shuāng xúnhuán)" strategy (hereinafter "DCS") (焦鹏 (Jiao Peng) 2020; Yao 2020; EIU 2020; Bhurtel 2020; Oya 2020).

Conceived as the renewal of Beijing's economic policy guidelines, the strategy was announced for the first time during the last May's Politburo meeting, and strongly re-launched at the end of July. As often happens in these cases, possible far-reaching transformations are hidden under a vague in content phrase. To prove the significance of the concept, it is of utmost importance to go over its fundamental elements. The starting point is the literal translation of "double circulation", which, in the vision proposed by President Xi Jinping, is understood as a dialectic between domestic and international economic circulation. To better grasp the concept, think that the Chinese term is the same used when talking about "blood circulation—血液循环 (xuèyè xúnhuán)". Making it easy, the global demand (external circulation) and household consumption (internal circulation) are set to be closely correlated. The dynamic to be managed is that between an economy dependent on exports and, therefore, on international demand, and a wider role granted to domestic consumption. Today's indication is that, in the current context of uncertainty, due to the pandemic and trade disputes, China's economy must chiefly focus on internal circulation.

DCS seems to determine a novel approach and, in this regard, the pandemic and the worsening of relations with the US come into play. The Chinese response to the impact of COVID-19, in fact, was aimed above all on the production side, thanks to the adoption of such measures as tax cuts and investments in infrastructure, while the negative repercussions of the pandemic have mainly spilled on consumption. This way, both inequality and the weight of international demand compared to domestic demand have increased. This links to the whole debate on the "decoupling", which is not primarily an American phenomenon but also concerns the Chinese will to reduce its own external dependence through the "self-reliance"–substantially, technological autarchy—that precedes Washington's reflections on its dependence on Beijing.

For these reasons, DCS can be sanctioned as a policy aimed at making the economy more resilient to external shocks, by promoting internal demand as its main driver (Trivium China 2020). The figure that catches the eye, in this area, is that of imports of integrated circuits which, with a value of more than 300 billion dollars, represent the first item of Chinese imports, exceeding the just under 250 billion dollars oil import, for which Beijing leads the world demand. Besides, investments in innovation (R&D) in 2019 also exceeded a growth rate of 10% (+12.5% compared to 2018), addressed, for around 82.7%–83.4%, to industrial development and, thus, contributing to the qualitative growth of Chinese industry (Normile 2020; Fasulo 2020).

If such a policy were actually pursued, while still following the trend lines sketched out for at least a decade, China would increasingly take the road to become more a land of consumption than production, thus favoring imports over exports and having at the same time reduced exposure to an increasingly hostile international context. But these measures must be adopted quickly, because, as mentioned, in recent months the Chinese trade surplus has continued to grow, reinforcing the circumstances that had led the Trump Administration to wage the trade war.

Nevertheless, the adoption of such measures raises two main issues in China. First, the achievement of greater internal consumption should pass through the transfer of resources to household consumption—retaining one of the lowest shares of GDP of any country in history. For Chinese consumption to be broadly in line with that of other developing countries, ordinary households should recover at least 10–15% points of GDP at the expense of businesses, the wealthy people, or the government. Indeed, this means reduced inequality, but at the same time, such kind of rebalancing involves a massive shift of wealth—and with it, political power—to ordinary people. Using a Chinese proverb, this will not be "as big as a sesame seed".

The second major problem is the internal contradiction at the heart of China's new "dual circulation" model. The export competitiveness of the country depends on ensuring that workers are allocated, whether by wages or the social safety net, a very low share of what they produce. China's export strength, in other words, depends, at least in part, on the low share workers retain of what they produce. Here is the problem: China can only rely on domestic consumption to drive a much greater share of growth if workers begin to receive a much higher share of what they produce, so the very process of rebalancing would undermine China's export competitiveness. This means that, for "internal circulation" to succeed, "international circulation" must be compromised. One cannot boost the other, as Beijing proposes: the shift itself will require a difficult adjustment period (Pettis 2020). It will therefore take years before the DCS reaches its goals, but the road seems to have been traced towards a China that is less dependent on foreign countries and more focused on its internal dimension, which is assumed to be a more relevant market.

However, the attention, in this case, must be maximum. DCS potentially represents the nerve center of the 14th Five-Year Plan (2021–2025) which will be approved in March 2021 and where, as stated in par. 1.2, Beijing will present itself at the new appointment as the only large economy to have achieved positive growth in 2020, and holding positive growth forecasts for the years ahead. This hypothesis found confirmation at the end of October 2020, when the Chinese Communist Party (CCP) held the 5th plenary session of the 19th Communist Party Central Committee,[17] unveiling the first glimpses of its economic plans for the next five years. Initial details released by the Communist Party's Central Committee, promised to build the nation into a technological powerhouse, as it emphasized quality growth over speed, vowed to achieve carbon neutrality ahead of 2060, stressed the need for sustainable growth, and also pledged to develop a robust domestic market.

Although no mention of the pace of growth policymakers would target was made, there was a distinct emphasis on strengthening the domestic economy since DCS was mentioned twice in the communique.[18] In particular, the nation needs to "smooth the domestic circulation, facilitate dual circulation at home and abroad, comprehensively promote consumption and expand room for investment," according to the statement. Thus, the plan will highlight the need to gain technological independence, elevating China's self-reliance onto a national strategic pillar, also in view of a prolonged trade war with the US; become a powerhouse in manufacturing, cyber, and the digital economy; raise China's international competitiveness; and prioritize ecological progress in every dimension and phase of economic and social development. At the same time, China will need to expand domestic consumption as a share of the economy, which will be

[17] The mandated annual convention of the full Central Committee of the Communist Party to assess the results of the previous Five-Year Plan (2016–2020) and consider the draft proposal for the next Five-Year Plan.

[18] The full communique is available at: http://www.xinhuanet.com/2020-10/29/c_1126674147.htm.

dependent on raising wages, building a more comprehensive social safety net, and expanding economic opportunities in rural China.

Indeed, a crucial point in the implementation of DCS is that it implies a structural change of the Chinese economic, social, and therefore, political context which must, at the same time, seek sustainability in those different domains (Di Tommaso et al. 2020a).

The sustainability of economic development implies the ability to manage a shift from an export-led model of growth to a domestic-demand-driven one. This would require addressing—first of all—issues related to people's propensity to consumption, which must be increased in the long run modifying typical and eradicated habits of Chinese people, while leveraging the consumption potential of the country's rural areas.

On the other side, supply-side reforms are fundamental, so as to: (a) keep high competitiveness of domestic firms in the light of the rush to innovation supremacy, and despite the trade war with the US; (b) further push the reform of State-owned enterprises to increase efficiency and transparency; (c) increase internal competition and contrast local oligopolies.

However, the economic sustainability of the ongoing structural change needs also social sustainability. It also needs to rebalance social and territorial disparities in crucial fields such as access to education and health, child and elderly care, as well as the provision of public goods, effective management of environmental issues.

In one word: managing the economic and social sustainability of the ongoing dynamics of structural change, imposed by the pandemic and by the government's DCS response, should be considered the main challenge facing post-pandemic China.

References

Alon, I., Fetscherin, M., & Gugler, P. (Eds.). (2011). *Chinese International Investments*. New York: Palgrave Macmillan.

Barbieri, E., Di Tommaso, M. R., & Huang, M. (2010). Industrial Development Policy and Innovation in Southern China: Government Targets and Firms' Behavior. *European Planning Studies, 18*(1), 83–105.

Barbieri, E., Di Tommaso, M. R., & Mattia, T. (2015). Politiche industriali selettive e settori strategici. Lo scenario e le scelte di Pechino. *L'industria Rivista di economia e politica industriale, 3*, 403–434.

Barbieri, E., Huang, M., Pi, S., & Tassinari, M. (2017). Restructuring the Production of Medicines: An Investigation on the Pharmaceutical Sector in

China and the Role of Mergers and Acquisitions. *International Journal of Environmental Research and Public Health, 14*(10), 1179.

Barbieri, E., Di Tommaso, M. R., Pollio, C., & Rubini, L. (2020). Getting the Specialization Right. Industrialization in Southern China in a Sustainable Development Perspective. *World Development, 126*, 104701.

Bellabona, P., & Spigarelli, F. (2007). Moving from Open Door to Go Global: China goes on the world stage. *International Journal of Chinese Culture and Management, 1*(1), 93–107.

Bhurtel, B. (2020). *'Dual Circulation' Strategy China's Message to US. Beijing is Signaling That It Will Adapt to Any Trade Policy the US Pursues in the Future.* Asia Times. Retrieved from https://asiatimes.com/2020/08/dual-circulation-strategy-chinas-message-to-us/.

Bianchi, P., & Labory, S. (2018). *Industrial Policy for the Manufacturing Revolution.* Cheltenham: Edward Elgar Publishers.

Bloomberg. (2020). *Infrastructure Will Be a Top Priority for China in 2020.* Bloomberg. Retrieved from https://www.bloomberg.com/news/articles/2020-05-22/china-drives-home-commitment-to-new-infrastructure-investment.

Buckley, P., Clegg, J., Cross, A., Liu, X., Voss, H., & Zheng, P. (2007). The Determinants of Chinese Outward Foreign Direct Investment. *Journal of International Business Studies, 38*, 499–518.

Central Committee of the Communist Party of China (CCCPC). (2016). *The 13th Five-Year Plan for Economic and Social Development of the People's Republic of China (2016–2020).* Central Compilation and Translation Press. Retrieve October 28, 2020, from https://www.un-page.org/files/public/china_five_year_plan.pdf.

Chaisse, J., & Matsushita, M. (2018). China's Belt And Road Initiative: Mapping the World Trade Normative and Strategic Implications. *Journal of World Trade, 52*(1), 163–185.

Chang, H.-J. (1994). *The Political Economy of Industrial Policy.* London and Basingstoke: Macmillan.

Chang, Y.-Y. (2019). Understanding the Belt and Road Initiative (BRI). *European Journal of East Asian Studies, 18*(1), 7–35.

Choi, Y. (2011). The Evolution of "Socialism with Chinese Characteristics": Its Elliptical Structure of Socialist Principles and China's Realities. *Pacific Focus, 26*(3), 385–404.

Chong, T. T. L., & Li, X. (2019). Understanding the China–US Trade War: Causes, Economic Impact, and the Worst-Case Scenario. *Economic and Political Studies, 7*(2), 185–202. https://doi.org/10.1080/20954816.2019.1595328. Retrieved from www.scopus.com.

Deng, X. (1985). *Build Socialism with Chinese Characteristics.* Foreign Languages Press.

Deng, P. (2009). Why Do Chinese Firms Tend to Acquire Strategic Assets in International Expansion? *Journal of World Business, 44*(1), 74–84.

Di Tommaso, M. R., & Schweitzer Stuart, O. (2013). *Industrial Policy in America: Breaking the Taboo.* Cheltenham England: Edward Elgar Publishers.

Di Tommaso, M. R., & Tassinari, M. (2014). Governo e Industria negli Stati Uniti. Le pratiche del passato e il dibattito sulle politiche del presente. *L'industria, 3*, 369–408.

Di Tommaso, M. R., Rubini, L., & Barbieri, E. (2013). *Southern China: Industry, Development and Industrial Policy.* Milton Park Abingdon: Routledge.

Di Tommaso, M. R., Pollio, C., Barbieri, E., & Rubini, L. (2019). Chinese Industrialization, Planning and Policies: Local Growth and Global Equilibria. In P. Bianchi, C. Ruiz Duran, & S. Labory (Eds.), *Transforming Industrial Policy for Digital Age: Production, Territories, and Structural Change.* Cheltenham: Edward Elgar Publishing.

Di Tommaso, M. R., Tassinari, M., & Ferrannini, A. (2020a). Industrial Policy and Societal Goals. A new look at the American case (from Hamilton to Obama and Trump). In S. Pressman (Ed.), *How Social Forces Impact the Economy.* Milton Park Abingdon United Kingdom: Routledge.

Di Tommaso, M. R., Spigarelli, F., Barbieri, E., & Rubini, L. (2020b). *The Globalization of China's Health Industry. Industrial Policies, International Networks and Company Choices.* London: Palgrave Macmillan.

Dirlik, A. (1989). Postsocialism? Reflections on "Socialism with Chinese Characteristics". *Bulletin of Concerned Asian Scholars, 21*(1), 33–44.

European Union Chamber of Commerce in China—EUCCC. (2017). *China Manufacturing 2025. Putting Industrial Policy Ahead of Market Forces.* EUCCC. Retrieved from http://www.cscc.it/upload/doc/china_manufacturing_2025_putting_industrial_policy_ahead_of_market_force%5Benglish-version%5D.pdf.

Fasulo, F. (2019, in press). International Cooperation for Industry Capacity as the Long Term Pillar of BRI: Opportunities and Obstacles.

Fasulo, F. (2020). Xi Jinping e la sua economia duale. *ISPI.* Retrieved from https://www.ispionline.it/it/pubblicazione/xi-jinping-e-la-sua-economia-duale-27361.

Ferdinand, P. (2016). Westward ho-the China Dream and 'One Belt, One Road': Chinese Foreign Policy Under Xi Jinping. *International Affairs, 92*(4), 941–957. https://doi.org/10.1111/1468-2346.12660. Retrieved from https://academic.oup.com/ia/article/92/4/941/2688105.

Garnaut, R., Song, L., & Fang, C. (2018). *China's 40 Years of Reform and Development: 1978–2018.* ANU Press.

Okamoto, G. (2020). *Securing China's Post-Pandemic Recovery: Deepening Reforms and Pursuing Rebalancing.* International Monetary Fund. Retrieved from https://www.imf.org/en/News/Articles/2020/09/24/sp092420-securing-china-s-post-pandemic-recovery.

GlobalData Healthcare. (2019). *US-China Trade War Casualties: Biopharma Sees the First Wave of CFIUS Vetoes, But No Tariffs on Chinese Pharma Imports.* Retrieved October 28m, 2020, from https://www.pharmaceutical-technology.com/comment/us-china-pharma-trade-2019/.

Gong, H., Hassink, R., Tan, J., & Huang, D. (2020). Regional Resilience in Times of a Pandemic Crisis: The Case of COVID-19 in China. *Tijdschrift voor Economische en Sociale Geografie, 111*(3), 497–512. https://doi.org/10.1111/tesg.12447.

Green, F., & Stern, N. (2015). *China's "New Normal": Structural Change, Better Growth, and Peak Emissions.* CCCEP and Grantham Research Institute on CGE. Retrievee from https://www.lse.ac.uk/GranthamInstitute/wp-content/uploads/2015/06/China_new_normal_web1.pdf.

Hammer, A. B. (2017). *'Made in China 2025' Attempts to Restimulate Domestic Innovations.* USITC Executive Briefings on Trade.

Hanemann, T., Huotari, M., & Kratz, A. (2019). *Chinese FDI in Europe: 2018 Trends and Impact of New Screening Policies.* Report by Rhodium Group and the Mercator Institute for China Studies (MERICS). Retrieved February 17, 2020, from https:/rhg.com/research/chinese-fdi-in-europe-2018-trends-and-impact-of-new-screening-policies/.

Hsu, J., Di, L., Ya Min, Y., Hui Tong, Z., Zhi Rou, C., Jiao, L., & Wei, C. (2016). The Top Chinese Mobile Health Apps: A Systematic Investigation. *Journal of Medical Internet Research, 18*(8), e222.

Huang, Y. (2016). Understanding China's Belt & Road Initiative: Motivation, Framework and Assessment. *China Economic Review, 40*, 314–321. https://doi.org/10.1016/j.chieco.2016.07.007. Retrieved from www.scopus.com.

Institute for Security & Development Policy—ISDP. (2018). *Made in China 2025 Backgrounder.* Retrieved October 31, 2020, from https://isdp.eu/content/uploads/2018/06/Made-in-China-Backgrounder.pdf.

International Monetary Fund—IMF. (2020a). *GDP, Current Prices.* International Monetary Fund. Retrieved October 28, 2020, from https://www.imf.org/external/datamapper/PPPGDP@WEO/OEMDC/ADVEC/WEOWORLD.

International Monetary Fund—IMF. (2020b). *IMF DATA—ACCESS TO MACROECONOMIC AND FINANCIAL DATA—Regional Economic Outlook: Asia and Pacific.* International Monetary Fund. Retrieved October 31, 2020, from https://data.imf.org/?sk=ABFF6C02-73A8-475C-89CC-AD515033E662&sId=1462204389301.

Kolstad, I., & Wiig, A. (2012). What Determines Chinese Outward FDI? *Journal of World Business, 47*, 26–34.

Layne, C. (2020). Preventing the China-U.S. Cold War from Turning Hot. *The Chinese Journal of International Politics, 13*(3), 343–385. https://doi.org/10.1093/cjip/poaa012. Retrieved from Oxford Academic.

Li, L. (2018). China's Manufacturing Locus in 2025: With a Comparison of "Made-in-China 2025 and Industry 4.0. *Technological Forecasting and Social Change, 135*, 66–74. https://doi.org/10.1016/j.techfore.2017.05.028. Retrieved from www.scopus.com.

Li., C, He, C., & Lin, C. (2018). Economic Impacts of the Possible China–US Trade War. *Emerging Markets Finance and Trade, 54*(7), 1557–1577. https://doi.org/10.1080/1540496X.2018.1446131. Retrieved from Taylor & Francis Online.

Li, H., Zhang, T., Chi, H., Chen, Y., Li, Y., & Wang, J. (2014). Mobile Health in China: Current Status and Future Development. *Asian Journal of Psychiatry, 10*, 101–104.

Ling, L., & Quan, H. (2017). The Logic of Long-Term Growth of China: From New Normal to Supply-Side Reform. *International Journal of China Studies, 8*, 2.

Liu, T., & Woo, W. T. (2018). Understanding the U.S.-China Trade War. *China Economic Journal, 11*(3), 319–340. https://doi.org/10.1080/17538963.2018.1516256. Retrieved from www.scopus.com.

Liu, W., Dunford, M. (2016). Inclusive Globalization: Unpacking China's Belt and Road Initiative. *Area Development and Policy, 1*(3), 323–340. https://doi.org/10.1080/23792949.2016.1232598. Retrieved from Web of Science.

Liu, W., & Zhang, H. (2019). *Global Economic Synergy of Belt and Road Initiative*. New York: Springer. ISSN: 2661-9105. Retrieved from: https://link.springer.com/bookseries/16304.

Lv, Q., Jiang, Y., Qi, J., Zhang, Y., Zhang, X., Fang, L., Tu, L., Yang, M., Liao, Z., Zhao, M., Guo, X., Qiu, M., Guieruo, J., & Lin, Z. (2019). Using Mobile Apps for Health Management: A New Health Care Mode in China. *JMIR Mhealth Uhealth, 7*(6), e10299.

Majumder, S., Tapas, M., & Deen, M. (2017). Wearable Sensors for Remote Health Monitoring. *Sensors, 17*(1), 130.

Meidan, M., Sen, A., & Campbell, R. (2015). *China: The 'New Normal'*. The Oxford Institute for Energy Studies. Retrieved from https://www.oxfordenergy.org/wpcms/wp-content/uploads/2015/02/China-the-new-normal.pdf.

Meinhardt, C. (2020). *China Bets on 'New Infrastructure' to Pull the Economy Out of Post-COVID Doldrums*. MERICS. Retrieved from https://merics.org/en/analysis/china-bets-new-infrastructure-pull-economy-out-post-covid-doldrums.

Misiągiewicz, J., & Misiągiewicz, M. (2017). *China's "One Belt, One Road" Initiative—The Perspective of the European Union*. Annales UMCS. Retrieved from https://journals.umcs.pl/k/article/view/3494/3628.

Müller, J. M., & Voigt, K.-I. (2018). Sustainable Industrial Value Creation in SMEs: A Comparison between Industry 4.0 and Made in China 2025. *International Journal of Precision Engineering and Manufacturing-Green*

Technology, 5, 659–670. https://doi.org/10.1007/s40684-018-0056-z. Retrieved from: Springer.

Newmarker, C. (2019). *The U.S.-China Trade-War: Here's What It Means for Medical Device Industry Suppliers*. Medical Design and Outsourcing. Retrieved from https://www.medicaldesignandoutsourcing.com/the-u-s-china-trade-war-heres-what-it-means-for-medical-device-industry-suppliers.

Normile, D. (2020). *China Again Boosts R&D Spending by More Than 10%*. ScienceMag. Retrieved from https://www.sciencemag.org/news/2020/08/china-again-boosts-rd-spending-more-10.

Oya, S. (2020). What China's 'Dual Circulation' Strategy Means for the World. *Japan Times*. Retrieved November 5, 2020, from https://www.japantimes.co.jp/opinion/2020/11/03/commentary/world-commentary/china-dual-circulation-strategy/.

Perskaya, V. V. (2019). "Made in China 2025" as a Tool for the Development of the Economic Model of Socialism with Chinese Characteristics. *Advances in Economics, Business and Management Research, 107*, 38–40.

Petti, C., Prota, F., & Rubini, L. (2016). Two Decades of Made in China Innovation. *L'industria, 37*(4), 565–585.

Pettis, M. (2020). The Problem With China's "Dual Circulation" Economic Model. *Financial Times*. Retrieved from https://ftalphaville.ft.com/2020/08/24/1598278946000/The-problems-with-China-s%2D%2DDual-Circulation%2D%2Deconomic-model/.

Poon, C. C. Y., Liu, Q., Gao, H., Lin, W.-H., & Zhang, Y.-T. (2011). Wearable Intelligent Systems for E-Health. *Journal of Computing Science and Engineering, 5*(3), 246–256.

Rees, V. (2019, June 18). *US-China Trade War Leaves Gap for Indian Pharma to Grow*. European Pharmaceutical Review. Retrieved from https://www.europeanpharmaceuticalreview.com/news/89905/us-china-trade-war-leaves-gap-for-indian-pharma-to-grow/.

Rodrik, D. (2008). *Normalizing Industrial Policy*. Commission on Growth and Development Working Paper, n. 3. Washington, DC: World Bank.

Saggu, A., & Anukoonwattaka, W. (2015). China's 'New Normal': Challenges Ahead for Asia-Pacific Trade. *United Nations ESCAP, 11*, 1–10.

Spigarelli, F. (2018). Politica industriale e cambiamenti strutturali: la via cinese alla crescita. *L'Industria, 4*, 511–522.

Spigarelli, F., & Ping, L. (2018). *The New Silk Road to Europe: Retrospect and Prospect of the Belt and Road Initiative 5 Years from Inception*. Working Paper, Ambrosetti House. Retrieved July 28, 2019, from https://www.ambrosetti.eu/summit-workshop-e-forum/summit-internazionali-con-think-tank/belt-and-road-2018/.

Staff Reuters. (2020). *China Takes Major Steps to Prop Up Coronavirus-Hit Economy*. Emerging Markets. Retrieved from https://www.reuters.com/

article/us-china-health-policy-factbox/china-takes-major-steps-to-prop-up-coronavirus-hit-economy-idUSKBN20E101.

The Economist Intelligence Unit. (2020). *Turning Inwards: What Asia's Self-Sufficiency Drive Means for Business and Investors.* The Economist Intelligence Unit. Retrieved from https://www.eiu.com/n/campaigns/turning-inwards/?utm_source=facebook&utm_medium=organic_social&utm_campaign=asia_turning_inwards&utm_term=domestic_economy&utm_content=graphic_2&linkId=100000015446599&fbclid=IwAR206Sgv5apz3jC0jm0BfFM2FggsdaGhADoucUylOYainOf9VDTbqa7mM04.

Trivium China. (2020). Dual Circulation Explained, Sort Of, Trivium China. Retrieved October 28, 2020, from https://triviumchina.com/2020/08/25/dual-circulation-explained-sort-of/.

UNCTAD. (2020). *Impact of the COVID-19 Pandemic on Global FDI and GVCs.* Special Issues. UNCTAD. Retrieved from https://unctad.org/news/coronavirus-could-cut-global-investment-40-new-estimates-show.

Wei, L. (2019). Towards Economic Decoupling? Mapping Chinese Discourse on the China–US Trade War. *The Chinese Journal of International Politics, 12*(4), 519–556. https://doi.org/10.1093/cjip/poz017. Retrieved from Oxford Academic.

Wong, D. (2019). Investing in China's Healthtech Industry. China briefing, 25.07.2019. Available at: https://www.china-briefing.com/news/investing-chinashealthtech-industry/.

World Bank. (2020a). *"From Containment to Recovery" East Asia and Pacific Economic Update (October).* Washington, DC: World Bank. https://doi.org/10.1596/978-1-4648-1641-3. License: Creative Commons Attribution CC BY 3.0 IGO. Retrieved from https://www.worldbank.org/en/region/eap/publication/east-asia-pacific-economic-update.

World Bank. (2020b). *China Economic Update, July 2020: Leaning Forward—COVID-19 and China's Reform Agenda.* Washington, DC: World Bank. © World Bank. License: CC BY 3.0 IGO. Retrieved from https://openknowledge.worldbank.org/handle/10986/34264.

World Trade Organization. (2020). Trade Set to Plunge as COVID-19 Pandemic Upends Global Economy. Retrieved from https://www.wto.org/english/news_e/pres20_e/pr855_e.htm.

Wübbeke, J., Meissner, M., Zenglein, M. J., Ives, J., & Conrad, B. (2016). *Made in China 2025: The Making of a High-Tech Superpower and Consequences for Industrial Countries.* Merics Paper on China. Retrieved July28, 2019, from https://kritisches-netzwerk.de/sites/default/files/merics_-_made_in_china_2025_-_the_making_of_a_high-tech_superpower_and_consequences_for_industrial_countries_-_76_seiten_1.pdf.

Xinhua. (2020a). *How Does China Combat #Coronavirus: Nearly 600 Policies Unveiled in 10 Days to Support Small Businesses.* Xinhua Net. Retrieved from http://www.xinhuanet.com/english/2020-02/25/c_138816121.htm.

Xinhua. (2020b). *Zoom-in: China's Supportive Measures to Enliven Economy Amid Epidemic.* Xinhua net. Retrieved from http://www.xinhuanet.com/english/2020-02/24/c_138814602.htm.

Xu, L. D., Xu, E. L., & Li, L. (2018). Industry 4.0: State of the Art and Future Trends. *International Journal of Production Research, 56*(8), 2941–2962. https://doi.org/10.1080/00207543.2018.1444806. Retrieved from www.scopus.com.

Yao, K. (2020). *What We Know About China's 'Dual Circulation' Economic Strategy.* Reuters. Retrieved from https://www.reuters.com/article/china-economy-transformation-explainer-idUSKBN2600B5.

Yu, H. (2017). Motivation Behind China's 'One Belt, One Road' Initiatives and Establishment of the Asian Infrastructure Investment Bank. *Journal of Contemporary China, 26*(105), 353–368. https://doi.org/10.1080/10670564.2016.1245894. Retrieved from: Web Of Science.

Zenglein, M.J., & Holzmann, A. (2019, July). *Evolving Made in China 2025. China's Industrial Policy in the Quest for Global Tech Leadership.* Merics Paper on China n. 8. Retrieved July 28, 2019, from https://www.merics.org/en/papers-on-china/evolving-made-in-china-2025.

Zhang, Y. (2020). *China to Introduce Strong Financial Measures to Help Smaller Firms Tide Over Difficulties.* The State Council of The People's Republic of China. Retrieved from http://english.www.gov.cn/premier/news/202002/25/content_WS5e5534dac6d0c201c2cbce84.html.

Zhang, W., Alon, I., & Lattemann, C. (2018). *China's Belt and Road Initiative. Changing the Rules of Globalization.* Palgrave Macmillan. https://doi.org/10.1007/978-3-319-75435-2. Retrieved from https://www.palgrave.com/gb/book/9783319754345?utm_campaign=SRCN_1_LL_bri19_en_b.

焦鹏 (Jiao Peng). (2020). 中共中央政治局常务委员会召开会议 习近平主持. *Xinhua Net.* Retrieved from http://www.xinhuanet.com/politics/2020-05/14/c_1125986000.htm.

CHAPTER 2

Can China Be Less Dependent on Exports?

Risto Herrala

Abstract Chinese export growth has slowed down dramatically during the past decade. While the slowdown in part reflects a shift in Chinese economic policies, it has been accompanied by significant international tensions. Chinese influence is increasingly resisted around the world, as indicated by the broadside of trade "wars" and boycotts faced by Chinese firms and products abroad. The chapter reviews the underlying tensions between China and its export partners and projects the Chinese path in the global economy.

Keywords Exports • Trade war • Economic growth

R. Herrala (✉)
Bank of Finland Research Institute for Emerging Economies (BOFIT), Helsinki, Finland
e-mail: risto.herrala@bof.fi

F. Spigarelli, J. R. McIntyre (eds.), *The New Chinese Dream*, Palgrave Studies of Internationalization in Emerging Markets, https://doi.org/10.1007/978-3-030-69812-6_2

2.1 Introduction

Chinese export growth has slowed down dramatically during the past decade. After outperforming just about every other country for decades with double digit growth rates and, eventually, becoming the largest goods exporter, the Chinese economy seems recently to have hit quicksand on the global arena. Even before the COVID-19 Pandemic, Chinese export growth rates had fallen to near insignificance by historical standards at just below four percent per annum. Chinese exports are no longer expanding relative to the size of the global economy (see Chart 2.1).

A slowdown in export growth was in the cards even before the actual numbers crept in against the background of the government's pursuit of a new growth model that focuses less on international competitiveness and more on developing the domestic economy. The shift in focus away from export—led growth could even be considered overdue, given that the new policy line was first announced already in 2006 at the National People's Congress (NPC) under the former president Hu's first term in power.

However, it would be optimistic to shrug off China's foreign trade slowdown merely as late implementation of the NPC 2006 policy line, given the significant international tensions associated with these developments. Based on the more recent events one cannot help wondering

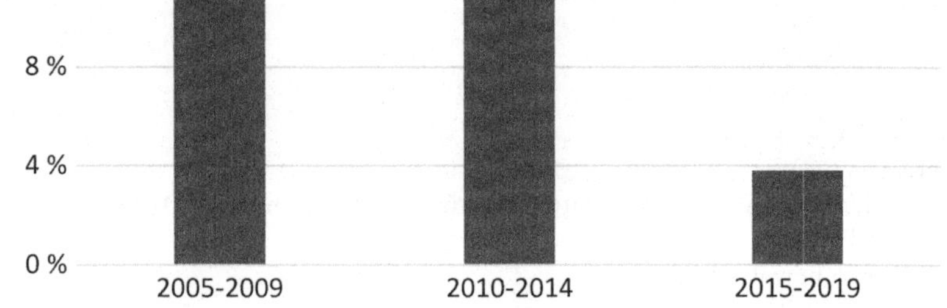

Chart 2.1 Export growth in China. (Notes: Average annual growth rate of Chinese total exports measured in CNY. Source: Macrobond)

whether something has gone amiss with the delivery of China's global economic agenda.

During the past years, Chinese trade relations with the rest of the world have become increasingly strained, or even critical. Exports from China and, more generally, Chinese influence is increasingly resisted around the world, as indicated by the broadside of trade wars and boycotts faced by Chinese firms and products abroad. What is going on?

2.2 China's Repositioning in the Global Economy

While China has during the past decades been hugely successful in gaining market share in labor-intensive sectors globally, the Chinese government has at the same time aspired to reposition China in the global arena towards higher value-added production: a strategy which has progressed impressively until late.

As anticipated in Chap. 1, in connection with the most recent national strategy review in 2015, this aspiration was formulated in terms of a goal to remake China from the factory floor of the world to a global innovator. This laudable vision of China's future global role is part of the "China Dream" launched by president Xi's government that calls on one hand for economic development and reform and, on the other, tight leadership of the ruling communist party. Within this general governance model, the Chinese leadership hopes to steer the country towards prosperity and, by the end of the first half of the century, towards the status of a leading global industrial power.

Over the past decades, the Chinese leadership has consistently worked to develop the Chinese economy towards this goal, by using the broad set of instruments at its disposal. One important development area has been scientific capacity building (see Chap. 3). China has sent its talent to study abroad *en masse*. As a result, over three hundred thousand Chinese students enroll each year in US universities alone, making the Chinese the largest foreign student group. At the same time, the Chinese government has worked to improve the education system at home. Consequently, many Chinese universities, most notably the Tsinghua University and the University of Peking, are ranked very high in international comparisons. As a concrete sign of success of creating and nurturing scientific talent, China became the top filer of patents in the world in 2019.

The Chinese leadership has also shown understanding that scientific progress is not sufficient alone to achieve the China Dream. Chinese firms also need to have the skill to put that knowledge to good use to develop, produce, and market new products both domestically and internationally. In this area, the Chinese have also made significant gains, as witnessed by the international surge in recent years of high-tech products such as mobile phones and telecom equipment, cars, games and mobile applications, and health care equipment from China (as described in the following Chapters of this book). To the dismay of many economists, the Chinese have achieved success with industrial policies that could be characterized as beefed up versions of those widely employed in other developing countries, rather than policies that are characteristic of the developed world.

2.3 Industrial Policies with Chinese Characteristics

During the early decades of reform and opening in the 1980's and 1990's, China eased restrictions on private sector enterprise, thereby creating the expectation that the Chinese economy was on its way to become a free market economy. However, during Hu Jintao's reign and increasingly so during Xi Jinping's ongoing terms in office, evidence has accumulated (Woo 2019; Herrala and Jia 2014) that the leadership instead wants to sustain a two-tier economic system, where state-owned enterprises (SOEs) and other politically affiliated companies receive preferential treatment from the government relative to politically weakly affiliated firms.

Under the Chinese system, success at firm level is therefore influenced not only by market forces, but also by politics. To be clear, SOEs and other state affiliated firms do play an important role also in many industrialized countries but, on this issue, China is on a league of its own. Based on an OECD survey of 40 countries (OECD 2017), China hosted over 51,000 SOEs against the sum total of under 2500 SOEs in the other 39 countries combined.

With its two-tier corporate sector, China has already managed to nurture a number of internationally successful high tech companies such as the information technology giant Huawei, a global leader in 5G technology which grabbed the status of largest mobile phone manufacturer from the Korean Samsung in 2020, and the retail giant Alibaba, which ships more packages per day that Amazon and, since 2019, has operations also outside China. The Chinese have furthermore made significant headway in building the infrastructure, including not only roads and airports but also labor and financial markets and institutions, to make sure that the top Chinese firms get the support they need to succeed in their efforts to climb the technology ladder.

Part of the Chinese strength in technology is due to its natural resources. China is helped in its pursuit of technological advancement by its dominance globally in rare earth mineral deposits, which are important ingredients of future technical devices. China currently produces over 80 percent of the group of 17 rare earth minerals globally, mostly in the Inner Mongolia region. Rare earth metals and alloys have special chemical properties that make them useful in many high-tech devices such as computers, rechargeable batteries, cell phones, catalytic converters, magnets, and fluorescent lighting.

2.4 Reaching Outward

The Chinese have also bought into foreign technologies and markets through foreign direct investment (FDI). While Chinese FDI is not transparent, it has clearly played a role in promoting technology transfer from western countries and opening markets for many Chinese companies. Successful examples include the Hong Kong headquartered companies Lenovo, which purchase of the PC arm of IBM in 2005 has helped it to develop into one of the top PC makers globally with an estimated quarter of all PC shipments; and Geely, which purchased the Swedish luxury automaker Volvo in 2010 and has nurtured it back into global expansion. During recent years, the Chinese have invested heavily in gaming with Tencent becoming one of the global leaders in the industry. In 2011, Tencent purchased Riot Games, the developer of the wildly popular League of Legends game, and in 2016 the majority of the highly profitable Supercell, which is best known for its popular mobile games. It also owns minority stakes in a number of other top of the line game makers, such as Blizzard and Ubisoft.

While the western markets have been important channels for China's technological development, it also benefits from close ties to the developing world. Chinese outreach towards developing countries has been loosely packaged under the 'Belt and Road' (BOR) umbrella launched in 2013 under president Xi Jinping's first term in office. Initially, BOR was marketed more narrowly as China's outreach towards the landlocked former silk road countries in Central Asia and the Caucasus, where the Chinese have been active in, among other things, building transportation channels and factories, and aiding in resource extraction. Subsequently, the term has increasingly become synonymous with Chinese involvement in the developing world.

China is involved in development projects in a broad set of developing and emerging economies not only in Asia, but also in Africa (see Chap. 5) and the Americas. To these countries, China provides expertise, finance, and resources for a broad variety of large-scale development projects, such as building roads, railways, and harbors, and natural resource extraction. In the neighboring Kazakhstan, for example, ongoing belt and road projects include a glass factory, a wind farm, and a petrochemical complex. From its developing country partners China gets in return raw materials, and also a market for some of its products that are suited for the developing market consumers.

2.5 Playing Hardball

It is well established that the Chinese have not shied away from also using less benign tactics to achieve their ambitions to climb the global technology ladder. China is frequently targeted by other countries with accusations of industrial spying and illegal copying of technologies, as well as forced technology transfer of foreign firms that want to enter the Chinese market. Chinese companies, enjoying broad based government support, have been blamed for competing unfairly in other countries against privately owned firms that do not receive similar support from their governments.

At the WTO, the Chinese have also at times been targeted with accusations of severely disturbing the global economy by dumping. For example, in 2020 the EU commission imposed provisional duties on stainless steel products from China as a response to dumping concerns. At present, the Chinese are the dominant producers of steel, with over 50% market share globally. The stainless-steel glut in China has its roots in the early millennium, when steel production received priority status by the government, and it was reformed to increase the production efficiency of steel mills. As a result, Chinese production capacity increased by six-fold between 2001–2010.

Since the start of its membership at the WTO, China has been respondent in 44 cases regarding breaches in WTO rules. In its recent report (USTR 2019) the US trade representative concludes, among other things, that

- China has repeatedly committed to refrain from forcible technology transfer from U.S. companies, but still continues the practice using market access restrictions, the abuse of administrative processes, licensing regulations, asset purchases, and cyber and physical theft;
- China has regularly used export and import substitution subsidies throughout the past two decades in various sectors of economic activity, such as automobiles, textiles, advanced materials, medical products and agriculture, despite explicit prohibitions in the WTO Agreement;
- China often deploys illegal export restraints, such as export quotas, export licensing, minimum export prices, export duties and other restrictions. China has used these illegal export restraints to generate cost advantages to downstream producers in China at the expense of foreign producers, thereby creating pressure on foreign producers to move their operations, technologies and jobs to China.

The USTR furthermore notes that China's retaliatory use of trade remedies highlights another unique issue that WTO members face when dealing with China—the threat of reprisal. According to the USTR, foreign companies are hesitant to speak publicly, or to be perceived as working with their governments to challenge China's trade policies or practices, because they fear retaliation from the Chinese state. As a further persistent problem USTR seen China's inadequate regulatory transparency. China disregards many of its WTO transparency obligations, which places its trading partners at a disadvantage and often serves as a cloak for China to conceal unfair trade policies and practices from scrutiny.

The EU and other developed countries have similar experience of Chinese practices, as indicated by their refusal to grant China market economy status under the WTO. When China joined the WTO in 2001, it entered into a 15-year transition period during which it was expected to transform its economy from a largely centrally planned system to a market economy. During that period, other countries had widened scope to protect against possible harmful dumping from China. The year 2016, during which the transition period was supposed to end, came and went without any fanfare about change in China's status: the EU, along with the US and a number of other countries, still does not view China as a market economy. In contrast, the problems generated by China's practices are as acute as ever, as also witnessed by the recent protective tariffs against steel products. China challenged EUs position on the issue at the WTO, but when the case was not progressing in its favor China allowed it to lapse earlier this year.

2.6 Escalation

During the recent years, the trade disputes between China and many of its trading partners have taken an ominous turn. After trade negotiations between the US and China failed, the trade war between the two kicked into high gear in 2018 as the US imposed significant tariffs on imports from China, with China responding in kind. The US has since then imposed bans on sale of vital parts and technologies to the Chinese telecom giant Huawei, and also limited the use of the Android operation system in Chinese mobile phones.

The US-China trade war is only one part of the widening conflict. Several countries, including the Anglo-Saxon countries and many Asian countries such as Japan, Singapore, Vietnam and the Philippines, have banned Chinese participation in 5G networks, with a number of countries including India, currently considering similar measures. The EU, in which many of Huawei's 5G projects are located, issued a warning earlier this year about security risks in 5G networks, and it has been recently looking into toughening its policy line. The 5G bans have largely been motivated by concerns about perceived security issues, such as the possibilities of spying, in information networks provided by Chinese companies.

Recently, India responded to the border conflict with China by banning a large number of Chinese computer applications used in India, including the popular social media app TikTok. Discussions are ongoing in the country about whether the ban should be extended also to apps made in other countries, if the respective developers have significant ties to China. Similar bans against TikTok and WeChat are in preparation also in the US. Large scale bans on Chinese applications could severely impact the social media and gaming industries globally, where China has during recent years become a major contributor and investor.

A number of countries have also tightened the rules of direct foreign investment in response to perceived security threats from China. In the US, the tightened FIRRMA rules came into effect in 2018. Japan followed suit in 2019, and India in 2020. Recently the US revoked the special status afforded to Hong Kong in response to Beijing's application of the new security law and pledged to impose sanctions on individuals and institutions that in its view contributed to the loss of Hong Kong's autonomous status.

These developments are followed with concern by international companies that have operations in China or dealings with Chinese firms. While no large-scale exodus of international companies from China has so far been seen, some surveys indicate that firms are concerned about the how Chinese decoupling from the global economy will impact their production processes and actively reconsidering their globalization strategies. Some countries are already actively promoting firms' plans to leave China: Earlier this year, the Japanese government started giving subsidies for firms to leave China, and many firms have already decided to use the opportunity. A similar system is in place in South Korea and plans are also under consideration by the US government.

2.7 The Assertive China

In developed countries, politics usually does not interfere that much with business decisions, but that principle does not apply to China. The outward image of China among firms and consumers of other countries, which contributes to their willingness to purchase Chinese products and work with Chinese partners, is therefore affected by how Chinese policies are perceived abroad.

Under president Xi, the role of political control has been strengthened in the Chinese economy and society, as also witnessed by the strong political emphasis embedded in the China Dream. While the Chinese political life is largely opaque to foreign inspection, the snippets seen from the outside appear deeply concerning especially for the people in the western world. The demonstrations and restriction of freedoms in Hong Kong; the haunting pictures of detention camps and widespread destruction of religious sites in Xinjiang; the apparent cultural and religious suppression in Tibet; the suppression of political expression and detention of political dissidents; and broad-based censorship of media and the internet all point to a repressive authoritarian political system.

Previously, the negative outside image of the Chinese political system was softened by China's skillful diplomacy, which emphasized the win-win nature of interactions with China. Those days seem to be gone, however, as the Chinese government has increasingly adopted a harsh, nationalistic tone in its dealings with other countries. The co-operative China has been replaced in the international arena by the bully China, which actively seeks confrontation with other countries to show its economic and military might. The recent headlines include an island dispute with Japan, the constant pressure on Taiwan, the South China Sea conflict with Vietnam, Brunei, Malaysia and the Philippines, the deadly border clash with India, the land grab in Nepal and the territorial dispute with the tiny Bhutan.

Moreover, China targets harshly countries that dare to criticize its policies, as widely covered in the international media. The various recent targets of Chinese 'wolf warrior diplomacy' include New Zealand, which the Chinese ambassador accused of gross interference in Chinese affairs for its reaction to the events in Hong Kong. New Zealand has for some time complained about serious issues with China including industrial spying and political interference. The Chinese have also recently threatened bad consequences for the Czech Republic for its support of Taiwan. Sweden was threatened by the Chinese ambassador after it awarded the Tucholsky prize to Gui Minhai, a Chinese dissident journalist. The neighboring Norway faced a backlash earlier for awarding the Nobel peace prize for Liu Xiaobo, a Chinese human rights activist, and Denmark for meeting with Tenzin Gyatso, the incumbent Dalai Lama, the Tibetan religious leader who lives in exile in India. The Chinese have also demonstrated willingness to take action towards countries that are critical of its policies. After years of largely turning a blind eye on Chinese political interference within its borders, Australia faced a backlash in the form of tariffs on barley and a ban on beef in China after suggesting that the origins of COVID-19 should be investigated by an international panel of experts.

Not only are such tactics likely to cause a political backlash, one that we are increasingly seeing around the world, but China is also constantly in the news in a bad way. The barrage of negative news is taking its toll on the image of China among the international consumer base. Based on surveys, a significant majority of consumers in the US have a negative impression of China (PEW 2020). In India, 90 percent of recent survey participants supported banning Chinese products (India Today 2020). In Japan, the sentiment is also overwhelmingly negative towards their large neighbor.

2.8 Chinese Global Economic Influence

While the day to day political and economic discourse provides ample evidence about negative changes in behavior and attitudes toward China, the science offers glimpse the big picture about whether the rise of the Chinese economy is, in fact, benefiting other countries or not. The related academic debate on this issue has during recent years also drifted gradually towards directions that cast China's global ambitions in less favorable light.

Inspired by the welfare theorems of economics, the mainstream positive attitudes on globalization and, in particular, China's rise in the global arena, have rested on the idea of mutual benefit. The argument at its core is that, eventually, everyone gains when China brings its considerable resources and talents to the service of humanity. These views receive indirect support from the various empirical studies, which show positive spillover from China to other countries (Dizioli et al. 2016; Feldkircher and Korhonen 2014; Arora and Vamvakidis 2011).

However, it has been argued that the empirical results, mainly building on the traditional econometric approaches such as the GVAR that use country level data, are not reliable for various, quite compelling, statistical reasons. Stronger identification is arguably achieved in studies with micro (firm level) data. Such studies reveal a less benign picture of Chinese influence in the global economy (Autor et al. 2016; Bloom and Draca 2016; Pierce and Schott 2016). They indicate that Chinese economic growth may cost jobs elsewhere, at least in the short run. This line of argumentation has been prominently voiced also among the policy circles during the trade wars.

Another strand of literature that casts a shadow on China's global rise are the studies that link Chinese economic expansion with the depletion natural resources (Herrala and Orlandi 2020; Zhuo 2018). The studies serve as reminder that an increase in economic growth in China leads to an increase in global commodity use and prices, thereby exerting a negative influence on welfare in other countries. Furthermore, China's massive demand of global commodities, fueled by its economic growth, has made it the largest greenhouse gas emitter, which alone emits more CO_2 than the EU and the US combined.

2.9 Where to from Here?

The concern that China is, indeed, in the process of decoupling from western markets is confirmed by the data of the geographical development of Chinese foreign trade. The data shows a sharp decline in Chinese exports to many developed markets in 2008–18, with the exception of the US, where exports stayed relatively flat (Chart 2.2). Based on the data, the Chinese star is therefore still shining in the developing world, especially among like-minded countries, but its gleam has vanished in the developed world.

One may only speculate about what lies ahead. Unfortunately, there does not seem to be much hope that the problems China is facing in its trade relations will vanish anytime soon. One factor pointing towards a prolonged conflict between China and its trading partners is that the complaints about China seem to be closely linked to its core political parameters. The opaqueness, nationalism, and drive for control of Chinese politics makes it difficult for China to regain the trust it needs to restore normal trade relations. Another factor that points to a prolonged conflict is that the resistance towards Chinese practices appears very widespread globally, encompassing the major developed and also many significant developing markets. In the past China has been skillful in curbing the resistance of

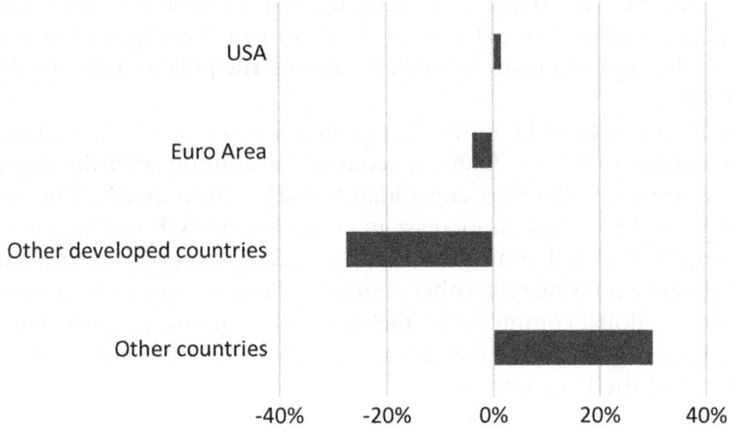

Chart 2.2 Chinese exports by area, change 2008–18, %. (Notes: The chart shows the difference in % points of export shares (of total exports) between 2018 and 2008. Data source: UN ComTrade)

individual countries that try to stand up to its bullying tactics. However, China's wolf warrior diplomacy does not work well against a widespread, powerful opposition.

A slowdown in exports and decoupling from the developed markets therefore seems ongoing and unlikely to vanish anytime soon. In the short run, the challenge for China is how to strengthen the domestic economy to compensate for the export slowdown, especially in the high-tech sector, while at the same time dealing with the pandemic. In the longer term, the Chinese leadership has to work out a credible path to the future to get China's populous and diverse nation to, again, march in line.

The path ahead therefore depends much on Chinese ambitions regarding their role in the global economy. The present path seems to be taking China towards a split world, where China is the technology champion mainly among like-minded countries in the developing world. For China to grow into a global technology leader that competes on equal footing with other countries would require real commitment to shared principles and willingness to address common issues in the global arena.

References

Arora, V., & Vamvakidis, A. (2011). China's Economic Growth: International Spillovers. *China & World Economy, 19*(5), 31–46.

Autor, D., Dorn, D., & Hanson, G. (2016). The China Shock: Learning from Labor Market Adjustment to Large Changes in Trade. *Annual Review of Economics, 8*, 205–240.

Bloom, N., & Draca, M. (2016). Trade-Induced Technical Change? The Impact of Chinese Imports on Innovation, IT, and Productivity. *Review of Economic Studies, 83*, 87–117.

Dizioli, A., Guajardo, J., Klyuev, V., Mano, R., & Raissi, M. (2016). *Spillovers from China's Growth Slowdown and Rebalancing to the ASEAN-5 Economies.* IMF Working Paper WP/16/170.

Feldkircher, M., & Korhonen, I. (2014). The Rise of China and Its Implications for the Global Economy: Evidence from a Global Vector Autoregressive Model. *Pacific Economic Review, 19*(1), 61–89.

Herrala, R., & Jia, Y. (2014). Toward State Capitalism in China, Asian. *Economic Papers, 14*(2), 163–175.

Herrala, R., & Orlandi, F. (2020). *Win-Win? Assessing the Global Impact of the Chinese Economy.* BOFIT discussion papers 4/2020.

India Today. (2020). *Mood of the Nation: 9 Out of 10 in Favor Of Boycotting Chinese Products.* Newspaper Article.

OECD. (2017). *Size and Distribution of State-Owned Enterprises, Presentation to OECD Steel Committee.*

PEW research center. (2020). *US Views on China Increasingly Negative Amid Coronavirus Outbreak.* Press Release.

Pierce, J., & Schott, P. (2016). The Surprisingly Swift Decline in US Manufacturing Employment. *American Economic Review, 106*(7), 1632–1662.

USTR (United States Trade Representative). (2019). *2018 Report to the Congress on China's WTO Compliance.*

Woo, W.-T. (2019). China's Soft Budget Constraint on the Demand-Side Undermines its Supply-Side Reforms. *China Economic Review, 57*, 1–8.

Zhuo, X. (2018). Study on the Interaction between International Commodity Price and China's Demand. *Chinese Studies, 7*, 34–46.

CHAPTER 3

Chinese Innovative Capacity—State of the Art of the Leading Edge

Peter Enderwick

Abstract To date technological catch-up by emerging economies such as China has been largely sequential, imitative, and achieved through established networks. However, attempts to achieve frontier technologies such as Industry 4.0 present significant new challenges impacting knowledge sources, knowledge types, transfer processes, and associated risks. This paper argues that to achieve this new level, Chinese firms will need to vary and widen the knowledge sources they utilize as they seek to develop both predictive capabilities (evaluating new technologies), and combinative capabilities (integrating them with the necessary skills and resources). Despite the deteriorating international business environment that it faces, China appears the best placed of all the major emerging economies to achieve this transformation.

Keywords Technological catch-up • Spill over • New technologies

---

P. Enderwick (✉)
AUT University, Auckland, New Zealand
e-mail: peter.enderwick@aut.ac.nz

F. Spigarelli, J. R. McIntyre (eds.), *The New Chinese Dream*, Palgrave Studies of Internationalization in Emerging Markets,
https://doi.org/10.1007/978-3-030-69812-6_3

3.1 Introduction

Attempts to explain sustained growth within many emerging economies are based on the concept of catch-up, that is emerging economies seeking to close the gap, primarily the technological gap, between themselves and the advanced or developed economies. The conceptual foundation of catch-up or convergence theory is that poorer countries, given the right conditions, can eventually match the income levels of more developed nations (Abramovitz 1986) through replication of the technologies, polices and institutions of successful predecessor nations.

Studies at the firm level reveal that learning involves significant effort highlighting the importance of learning processes as the foundation for capability building. Learning is deliberate, purposive, cumulative, and costly (Malerba 1992). Adequate absorptive capacity is critical for integrating and coordinating disparate knowledge sources. Catch-up learning is a circular rather than a linear process; one in which the firm must invest to both prepare for knowledge acquisition, and to ensure the effective absorption and transformation of external knowledge (Kim 1998).

This body of work provides some important insights. The first is a recognition of the importance of foreign technology and knowledge. Catch-up is based on a globally hierarchical structure of technology with leading or frontier technologies pioneered in developed countries and then (possibly) transferred to emerging economies. Second, research highlights the role of networks and linkages in facilitating transfer (Hertenstein et al. 2017). Network membership is an asset for the firm when it provides knowledge not available to outsiders. A third finding is the recognition that firms seeking to move from imitative to innovative learning need to both vary and widen the sources of knowledge that they utilize (Kotabe and Kothari 2016).

Continuing catch-up assumes the existence of appropriate conditions for accessing foreign technology: access to knowledge-rich networks, opportunities for broadening knowledge sources as new capabilities become critical, and the ability of domestic firms to modify and apply such knowledge to achieve commercial returns on knowledge investments. While such conditions may have existed for emerging economies such as China from around 1990 with the rise of the recent globalisation wave, changes in the global economy mean that such conditions can no longer be taken for granted. Three sets of developments are relevant to our discussion and relate to deteriorations in the international business environment for Chinese business, the impact of the Covid-19 pandemic, and the changing emphasis of Chinese development policies.

The past four years have seen significant changes in the global economy with a marked slowdown in trade levels, FDI flows, and global value chain growth (UNCTAD 2020). International trade has been characterised by rising disarray with the rejection of trade agreements and of trade disputes resolution. These disputes are linked to the ongoing trade war between China and the United States, which in turn seems to form part of a challenge to global economic hegemony (Witt 2019). A similar deterioration is also apparent with regard to foreign direct investment as a number of countries including Australia, the United States, the EU and India have tightened their screening of inward investment, particularly Chinese investment, raising concerns over national security, state-ownership of investors, and opportunistic acquisitions of distressed assets (Velten 2020; Doshi and Udgata 2020). In addition, in 2017 the Chinese authorities introduced greater scrutiny and some restrictions on Chinese outward FDI to avoid high risk and irrational investments and to better manage foreign exchange reserves, impacting cross-border M&As (Baker McKenzie 2018). A further adverse environmental change has been the imposition by the United States of direct restrictions on the operations of Chinese firms including Huawei and TikTok who have been denied market and technology access for reasons of national security. Other countries including Australia, Japan and Taiwan have adopted similar limitations on contracts available to Huawei. TikTok has suffered censorship bans in India and Indonesia, while the United States has voiced concerns over possible data sharing by the app.

A second environmental change likely to impact China's technological upgrading is the COVID-19 Pandemic. This is having several negative effects. The global paralysis will see falls in both trade and international investment to China, as well as outward investment of Chinese firms. Curtailment of international investment limits technology transfer and acquisition opportunities. Second, the costs of response to the pandemic may constrain the amount of R&D funds that Chinese firms and government organisations are able to commit to R&D, again slowing the development of absorptive capacity and the ability to develop new technologies. The resulting VUCA (volatility, uncertainty, complexity, and ambiguity) environment is likely to adversely affect innovation efforts through a reduction in funding, including venture capital funds, a slowdown in new product innovation, and fewer opportunities to achieve commercial returns on R&D investments. If the recovery leads to a restructuring of the recent hyper-globalisation wave, perhaps favouring a more regionally focused world economy (Enderwick and Buckley 2020), Chinese firms may have to forge new, more regionally focused networks for knowledge transfer. Direct partnerships may also be reduced where foreign governments provide incentives or directives for their firms to reshore or lessen dependency on Chinese operations (Bloomberg 2020; Rapoza 2020).

Third, conceptions of catch-up appear to be changing within China as the authorities move to achieve greater self-sufficiency. This is reflected in policy initiatives, mentioned in Chap. 1, such as Made In China 2025 which implies a greater level of domestic innovation by then, and the external focus of the Belt and Road Initiative that emphasises infrastructure rather than innovation investment for many leading Chinese firms. Critically, adoption of the new production technologies will require a much greater importance placed on knowledge acquisition and development and a significant broadening and deepening of absorptive capacity.

The aim of this chapter is to examine the opportunities and challenges that Chinese firms are likely to face when adopting the frontier production technologies described as Industry 4.0 (Lu 2017) and the factors likely to determine successful adoption. Given the insights offered (Bell and Figueiredo 2012), it is important to assess the value of catch-up theory in the context of Industry 4.0 knowledge. Industry 4.0 technologies, coalescing around advanced digitally-based production processes, represent both an opportunity and a challenge. The opportunity is the power to maintain manufacturing competitiveness in the face of rising labour and other costs, and the growing threat of backshoring as robotization and related technologies impact cost and locational advantages, and supply chain effectiveness. In addition, Industry 4.0 offers adopters flexibility and customisation advantages that consumers increasingly value.

However, the challenges are also considerable. Industry 4.0 technologies are disruptive: they have the potential to dramatically alter production processes and value adding. They also represent a departure for emerging market firms that have relied on traditional catch-up. The conditions for sourcing, assimilating, and exploiting Industry 4.0 are likely to be radically different from previous generations of product and process technologies. Of all emerging economies, China appears to display conditions most conducive to competitive success in advanced manufacturing processes.

The discussion in this chapter offers a contribution in several areas. First, there is limited work on the adoption of complex and disparate technologies as part of the catch-up process (Park 2013). As indicated earlier, the traditional view is of incremental, imitative, slow cycle learning of mature technologies (Zhou et al. 2017). The opportunity to leapfrog technologies has been seen as a selective strategy, variously described as innovative or path-creating, and pursued by relatively few emerging market firms. Industry 4.0 offers a disruptive technology that matches the manufacturing aspirations of China.

Second, traditional approaches to catch-up envision a sequential process where initial mastery focuses on process technologies before product and innovative technologies. However, the complex nature of Industry 4.0 technologies means that innovation and mastery of process technologies occurs simultaneously, not sequentially (Lee et al. 2014). This is a novel aspect examined in this chapter.

Third, the chapter provides an overview of Industry 4.0 adoption illustrating the distinct characteristics that are likely to be critical in making a successful transition.

To achieve the aim, the discussion is organised into four substantive sections. Following this introduction, we provide a brief overview of Industry 4.0 technologies and the challenges they present for adopters. Building on these, Section 3.3 discusses firm-level capability development in the implementation of Industry 4.0. Concluding comments are offered in Section 3.4.

3.2 Industry 4.0 and Challenges of Adoption

Industry 4.0 (the Fourth Industrial Revolution), is a generic term covering the growing digitalization of products, processes, and business models. The key transformation is the growing integration of production technologies (automation, additive manufacturing), and services encompassing data collection, storage, analysis, and application (Ustundag and Cevikcan 2018). The result is the increased connectivity of products, machines, workers, consumers and supply chains, the so-called 'Internet of Things'. Industry 4.0 is disruptive in that it changes conventional notions of production, supply, buyer behaviour, and organisational structures. Perhaps the most fundamental challenge that Industry 4.0 will bring is the importance of partnerships and relationships as organisations seek to integrate numerous, disparate, and rapidly evolving technologies (Kagerman et al. 2016).

The challenges that revolve around the knowledge characteristics of Industry 4.0 can be usefully grouped into four areas: knowledge type; knowledge sources; transfer processes; and risks. First, Industry 4.0 will mean major changes in the type of knowledge required. To date catch-up has relied on knowledge using, that is latecomer firms acquiring and applying existing knowledge. However, the fragmented nature of Industry 4.0 technologies will also require knowledge changing capabilities (Morrison et al. 2008). In the same way, while previous catch-up has drawn on existing production knowledge, adoption of Industry 4.0 will involve frontier knowledge that is new to the world. Not only is this knowledge novel, it is also layered, linking hardware such as sensors and control devices, to software including data processing, storage, and analytics.

The second challenge relates to the sources of knowledge under Industry 4.0. Previous catch-up has relied heavily on knowledge transfers from partners (through contractual outsourcing or co-production arrangements), competitors (through spillovers from inward FDI), and from technology acquisitions (outward FDI). In cases where production or assembly was outsourced, the standard production technologies were usually held and shared by lead firms responsible for industry GVCs. Industry 4.0 involves a much wider range of technologies controlled by disparate organisations including the large industrial integrators such as Siemens, GE and Hitachi, software developers (SAP, Microsoft), IT service providers (TCS, Infosys), and cloud infrastructure providers (AWS, Google) (Frederick et al. 2018). Much of the required technologies will be in the form of services, often highly knowledge-intensive. Adaptation of these technologies may no longer be the sole responsibility of the user but will necessitate complex networks and partnerships through open innovation.

Third, knowledge transfer processes will change under Industry 4.0. Well defined pipelines along global value chains or with established partner organisations will give way to a broader array of networks, formal and informal. Forced technology transfer achieved through joint ventures, knowledge transfer stipulations, or as a condition of market access will diminish in importance. One-way knowledge flows from innovator to follower will become increasingly reciprocal as emerging market firms gain complementary competences from product and technology adaptation, increased consumer understanding, and dynamic upgrading in the areas of quality, design, and speed to market.

Fourth, considerable risks will need to be managed. These include the danger of lock-in to obsolete or inoperable technologies, the existence of competing technological standards, and government restrictions on the operation of markets for resources. All of these challenges highlight the necessity to invest in building absorptive capacity within the firm. They also underscore the importance of complementary competences: in both anticipating change and what this means for technological scanning; and in integrative capabilities to bring together technologies of different types, from diverse sources, and to bridge technological discontinuities. These considerations are outlined in the following section.

3.3 Developing Innovative Capability for Industry 4.0

An important finding from the catch-up literature is recognition that firms seeking to move from imitative to innovative learning need to both vary and widen the sources of knowledge that they utilize (Gao 2018; Kotabe and Kothari 2016; Lema et al. 2018). The key benefit of employing a wider set of knowledge sources is that they enable the development of both predictive and combinative capabilities (Ahuja et al. 2005; Helfat and Peteraf 2003). Predictive capability is the ability to foresee, assimilate, and evaluate new knowledge in innovative ways allowing the firm to maximise new opportunities, earning higher returns on resources (Barney 1986). Familiarity with recent technologies enhances technological predictability (Katila 2002). Predictive capability is of particular value for technologies with a short life cycle. Within such technologies, incumbents may be locked-in and face switching costs (Dosi 1982), while latecomers have the opportunity to upgrade quickly.

Combinative facility is a dynamic capability enabling adaptation through the novel combination of resources and skills (Helfat and Peteraf 2003) offering sustained competitive advantage. Technological combinative capability enables the firm to move between technological generations, contributing to both adaptability (Mathews and Cho 1999) and ambidexterity (Liao et al. 2018). However, investment in combinative or explorative capabilities must be balanced with exploitation of existing knowledge (Gupta et al. 2006), and the deepening of absorptive capacity (March 1991).

Historically, catch-up has relied heavily on exploitative learning that occurs through the application of existing technologies and their incremental transformation within current products and uses. Knowledge exploitation occurs within what might be termed dense networks of linkages. These involve specialised and relatively narrow sets of relationships that provide the latecomer firm with cumulative experience with existing technologies. Such experience is a prerequisite for successful identification of new and emerging technological opportunities. The ability to develop exploitative capability is linked to investments in building and developing these networks. While there are numerous sources of exploitative knowledge, we highlight three of the most significant for China: market growth; export growth; and the rise of industry-specific clusters.

Strong market growth provides opportunities for exploitative learning as the size, growth rate and emergence of new market segments offers new applications. Economies of scale and learning by doing benefit from the existence of large or rapidly growing markets, while the development of new niches, perhaps pioneered by the firm, enable incremental knowledge transformation to occur as new applications or product traits are discovered.

Export growth, providing access to overseas markets, is also conducive to learning. Selling overseas exposes the firm to consumers with differing levels of sophistication, nascent market niches, as well as how to do business in diverse cultures. It may also open the firm to wider levels and types of competitors, providing useful insights into alternative sources and applications of knowledge. More generally, the firm faces different operating environments with institutional diversity, all of which contribute to the development of predictive powers. Indeed, such learning is at the heart of incremental internationalisation models, whether through participation in new markets or cross border networks.

The third source is business clusters, particularly those comprising industry- or technology-related groups of firms (Lorenzen and Mudambi 2013). Clustering facilitates interactive learning and increases exposure to novel forms and applications of relevant technologies (De Marchi et al. 2017). The development of higher levels of trust within established clusters may reduce knowledge transmission costs and increase access to tacit knowledge. Further opportunities may be available when such clusters expand, and inter-cluster connections develop.

The three market characteristics discussed here provide the greatest opportunities for developing predictive capabilities. The importance of investing in technological scanning is high at the present time. The geographical shift of manufacturing towards Asia, the growing servitization of manufacturing processes, the rise of short-cycle technologies, and the dangers of erroneous lock-in through technological leapfrogging, all highlight the need for predictive capabilities.

While developing predictive capabilities may be a necessary condition for the implementation of disruptive technologies, it is not a sufficient one. Also necessary are augmented combinative capabilities. In contrast to predictive capability that emphasises exploitative learning, combinative capabilities are developed using broad, explorative networks. Combinative abilities are formed through the recombination of existing resources and abilities (Kogut and Zander 1992). They enable the incorporation of incremental innovations and disruptive technologies through dynamic integrative learning. In essence, they allow latecomers to break free of technological dependence on others, and to avoid continuing reliance on established processes and routines.

An essential feature of successful exploratory networks is their diversity. Variety increases the likelihood of observing novel forms and applications of technology. Diversity of sources is a particular concern for emerging markets that generally lack the breadth of knowledge available in developed economies.

China has four primary networks conducive to the augmentation of combinative skills. The first is provided by diaspora and in particular returnees, individuals with experience of foreign countries attracted back to rapidly evolving emerging markets. Such individuals provide a valuable source of knowledge in part because they act as international knowledge brokers able to bridge knowledge gaps. Returnees may also have the advantage of early access to new knowledge, potentially contributing to both predictive and combinative capabilities. One of the key attractions of returnees is their ability to recontextualise knowledge, that is, to see knowledge in new ways and with new meanings in different cultural contexts. Larger established firms may be the more attractive structure for exploiting returnee's knowledge than an entrepreneurial venture when complementary assets are important, rare, specialised or tightly held (Rothaermel 2001).

A second network source of combinative skills is provided by participation in global value chains. While the technology provided by lead firms to contract producers within GVCs is typically mature, assistance in upgrading brings exposure to a wider range of skills. GVC networks are conducive to combinative skill development for two main reasons. The first is that if lead firms provide the incentives for upgrading and skill development, they are likely to transfer knowledge in areas of their comparative strength such as product and marketing competences, rather than process technologies that are usually outsourced. This increases the likelihood of access to knowledge complementary to the production skills of contract suppliers, assemblers, or manufacturers (Pietrobelli and Startiz 2018). Second, upgrading success appears to depend on access to complementary skill sets both internal to the value chain (other suppliers, customers) and external (local clusters, research institutes).

A third widely-researched knowledge transfer channel is that offered by inward foreign direct investment (IFDI). Emerging market firms may benefit from involvement with investors from developed economies either directly (through joint ventures for example), or indirectly, from externalities or spillover effects. Direct linkages have been used by several emerging economies, most notably China, to encourage the sharing of technologies, requiring joint ventures as a prerequisite for foreign firm access to the burgeoning home market. Indirectly, spillovers can occur though a number of mechanisms including demonstration effects, competition effects, and labour turnover.

The fourth combinative knowledge channel is outward foreign direct investment (OFDI). Such investments assume different forms ranging from R&D listening posts (Knoerich 2012) through to strategic asset seeking acquisitions (Dunning and Lundan 2008). OFDI offers several advantages as a mode for knowledge acquisition. It enables the precise targeting of desired assets or capabilities including technology, management skills and market access. These resources may not be available in open markets or may be difficult to transfer at arm's length given their tacit nature. It also enables targeting of unique knowledge, knowledge that is embedded within a nation's social and cultural context. Highly specific targeting offers an effective way to redress knowledge deficits, both technological and non-technological. Cross-border acquisitions also offer a speedy way to access capabilities that may be transferred and assimilated at a faster rate than attempting to develop them internally. Irrespective of the formality of linkage of OFDI, investing firms can gain knowledge in several ways. These include exposure to more sophisticated competitors in the host market, opportunities to exchange information with entities at different stages of the value chain such as final consumers, and through the attraction of local labour offering new knowledge sets. However, like the other channels of knowledge acquisition, successful OFDI assumes an appropriate level of absorptive capacity, both nationally within the home market, and within the individual firm. A well educated workforce and sound institutions facilitate transfer and use of knowledge, while at the firm level, prior experience with knowledge acquisition and assimilation are important (Makino et al. 2002).

Efforts to tap into these various channels for building predictive and combinative capabilities do not exist in isolation, they are moderated at both the national level through supportive government policies and the evolution of the national innovation system, and at the firm level through continuing investment in R&D and related skills. China has long implemented supportive policies to assist firm upgrading. Carefully targeted policies can assist local firm learning through the attraction of investors, enabling technology imports, and in permitting asset-seeking cross-border acquisitions. There is some evidence that the firms most successful at catch-up are those with a broad range of competencies (Gao 2018).

Analysis of the channels identified in the discussion highlight the advantages that China possesses with regard to Industry 4.0 technologies. In the early years following liberalisation China benefited from the inflow of work from Overseas Chinese, particularly those in Hong Kong and Taiwan attracted by lower costs and a future market. China has also been highly successful in attracting both contract manufacturing and assembly work in addition to inward foreign direct investment. Early requirements on market entry through joint ventures facilitated learning from partner organisations. More recently Chinese firms have been aggressively pursuing asset-seeking investments into developed economies (Deng 2007).

In the creation of predictive capabilities China benefits from a huge, rapidly growing and increasingly sophisticated market which is a pioneer in areas such as alternative energy sources, mobile payment systems, and high speed trains. Its export success is unprecedented, being the world's leading export nation. It also enjoys significant clusters involving public and private firms, government institutions, universities and research institutes focusing on sectors as diverse as golf products and eye wear (Zeng 2010).

China has other characteristics that make it a strong potential host for Industry 4.0 technologies. These include its robust and broad industrial base, its strong digital, internet and platform companies, the preponderance of private sector R&D activity, its ability to tap into complementary skills and resources within the Asian region, particularly within Japan, Korea and Taiwan, and its growing data economy. Many of its major firms enjoy strong government support, particularly with regard to upgrading, while China also retains other options for tackling issues of rising cost and the middle income trap, with opportunities to offshore labour intensive activities to less developed locations such as Vietnam and Cambodia.

The institutional structure and policy management approaches within China create traits associated with a coordinated economy, characteristics that facilitate the implementation of disruptive and complex technologies requiring corresponding approaches to regulation, standard setting, competition policy and skill requirements (Hall and Soskice 2001). China has also moved beyond early stage catch-up exemplified by technological imitation and given its market size and production capabilities is now capable of influencing or determining global industry standards. Combined, these attributes give China the ability to effectively leapfrog technologies with a high probability of targeting appropriate technologies (predictive capabilities) and of creating and protecting initial markets through large market size, supportive government policies, and the determination of industry standards (combinative capabilities).

3.4 Conclusions

This chapter has applied catch-up theory to the complex and disruptive technologies of Industry 4.0. It has highlighted the distinctive characteristics of these technologies and how they will require adopters to build absorptive capacity through significant investments in predictive and combinative capabilities. In contrast to the sequential, phase-based learning of past catch-up, Industry 4.0 requires compressed integrated learning around short-cycle technologies making knowledge prediction and combination fundamental. It necessitates innovative or path-creating learning as opposed to imitative or duplicative learning, the focus of traditional catch-up. Learning under Industry 4.0 adoption emphasises knowledge integration from disparate sources and the synergistic combination of internal and external knowledge channels. It also requires an effective balance between explorative and exploitative learning. The critical step in the assimilation of Industry 4.0 technologies will be the ability of Chinese firms to develop new broader and more diverse knowledge sources, and to assume greater responsibility in the integration of disparate technologies. Unfortunately, this comes at a time when China's international economic autonomy is being curtailed.

Despite the considerable competitive advantages possessed by China, these are the challenges that must be addressed. The reality is that some of the key technologies are dominated by the United States and deteriorating trade relations between the two countries have seen restrictions on technology transfer. The same argument applies to China's relations with Japan and India which need to be strengthened.

Second, China will need to re-evaluate its restrictions on data exchange, interoperability, and open innovation. Its leading internet companies Alibaba, Baidu, and Tencent, while very large companies, are predominantly focused on the domestic market. Adoption of Industry 4.0 production systems will require much more data exchange and a relaxation of the firewall restrictions.

It is also worth noting that to date, China and other leading economies in Asia have been complementary in their development of telecommunications and related technologies, but successful adoption of Industry 4.0 would place China in a dominant economic position within the region. This could create further tensions. Despite these concerns China appears to be the emerging economy most likely to dominate future process technologies.

While our discussion has contributed to catch-up thinking and its applicability in the contemporary context, there are several areas where further work is required. Given the importance of the state and state policies in this area there is a need to carefully develop the policy implications of our discussion. This is beyond the scope of the present paper, but the key issues revolve around the appropriate types, degree, and timing of policy interventions. Second, at the level of the firm we would benefit from work examining how latecomer learning strategies change over time, how knowledge sources change, and how combinative capabilities can be maintained. Third, Industry 4.0 brings short-cycle disruptive technologies to the forefront challenging catch-up theory that has historically focused on phase-based imitative product and functional upgrading, over process technologies. This indicates the need for further theoretical development.

References

Abramovitz, M. (1986). Catching-Up, Forging Ahead, and Falling Behind. *Journal of Economic History, 46*(2), 385–406.

Ahuja, G., Coff, R. W., & Lee, P. M. (2005). Managerial Foresight and Attempted Rent Appropriation: Insider Trading on Knowledge of Imminent Breakthroughs. *Strategic Management Journal, 26*(9), 791–808.

Baker McKenzie. (2018). *Rising Tension: Assessing China's FDI Drop in Europe and the United States.* Berlin: Baker McKenzie/Rhodium Group.

Barney, J. (1986). Strategic Factor Markets: Expectations, Luck, and Business Strategy. *Management Science, 32*(10), 1231–1241.

Bell, M., & Figueiredo, P. N. (2012). Innovation Capability Building and Learning Mechanisms in Latecomer Firms: Recent Empirical Contributions and Implications for Research. *Canadian Journal of Development Studies, 33*(1), 14–40.

Bloomberg. (2020, April 9). Japan to Pay Firms to Leave China, Relocate Production Elsewhere as Part of Coronavirus Stimulation. *Bloomberg News*.

De Marchi, V., Di Maria, E., & Gereffi, G. (Eds.). (2017). *Local Clusters in Global Value Chains: Linking Actors and Territories Through Manufacturing and Innovation*. London: Routledge.

Deng, P. (2007). Investing For Strategic Resources and its Rationale: The Case of Outward FDI From Chinese Companies. *Business Horizons, 50*(1), 71–81.

Doshi, H., & Udgata, S (2020, July 27). *India's Blueprint For Tackling Opportunistic Acquisitions During COVID-19 With Chinese Firms in Mind*. Columbia FDI Perspectives No 283.

Dosi, G. (1982). Technological Paradigm and Technological Trajectories: A Suggested Interpretation of the Determinants and Directions of Technical Change. *Research Policy, 11*(3), 147–162.

Dunning, J. H., & Lundan, S. M. (2008). *Multinational Enterprises and the Global Economy*. Edward Elgar Cheltenham.

Enderwick, P., & Buckley, P. J. (2020). Rising Regionalization: Will the Post-COVID-19 World See a Retreat From Globalization? *Transnational Corporations, 27*(2), 1–14.

Frederick, S., Bamber, P., & Cho, J. (2018). *The Digital Economy, Global Value Chains and Asia*. KIET/Duke Global Value Chains Center, Duke University.

Gao, X. (2018). Effective Strategies to Catch Up in the Era of Globalization. *Research-Technology Management, 61*(3), 19–26.

Gupta, A. K., Smith, K. G., & Shalley, C. E. (2006). The Interplay Between Exploration and Exploitation. *Academy of Management Journal, 49*(4), 693–706.

Hall, P. A., & Soskice, D. (2001). *Varieties of Capitalism: The Institutional Foundations of Comparative Advantage*. Cambridge: Cambridge University Press.

Helfat, C. E., & Peteraf, M. A. (2003). The Dynamic Resource-Based View: Capability Lifecycles. *Strategic Management Journal, 24*(10), 997–1010.

Hertenstein, P., Sutherland, D., & Anderson, J. (2017). Internationalization Within Networks: Exploring the Relationship Between Inward and Outward FDI in China's Auto Components Industry. *Asia Pacific Journal of Management, 34*(1), 69–96.

Kagerman, H., Anderl, R., Gausemeier, J., Schuh, G., & Wahlster, W. (Eds.). (2016). *Industrie 4.0 in a Global Context: Strategies for Cooperating with International Partners*. Munich: Herbert Utz Verlag.

Katila, R. (2002). New Product Search Over Time: Past Ideas in their Prime? *Academy of Management Journal, 45*(5), 995–1010.

Kim, L. (1998). Crisis Construction and Organizational Learning: Capability Building in Catching-Up at Hyundai Motor. *Organization Science, 9*(4), 506–521.

Knoerich, J. (2012). The Rise of Chinese OFDI in Europe. In I. Alon, M. Fetscherin, & P. Gugler (Eds.), *Chinese International Investments* (pp. 175–211). Basingstoke: Palgrave Macmillan.

Kogut, B., & Zander, U. (1992). Knowledge of the Firm, Combinative Capabilities, and the Replication of Technology. *Organization Science, 3*(3), 383–397.

Kotabe, M., & Kothari, T. (2016). Emerging Market Multinational Companies' Evolutionary Paths to Building a Competitive Advantage from Emerging Markets to Developed Countries. *Journal of World Business, 51*(5), 729–743.

Lee, A., Hannigan, T. J., & Mudambi, R. (2014, January 15–17) *Catch-Up in Technological Capability: A Comparison Between Korea and Brazil*. Paper presented at the DRUID Academy Conference, Aalborg.

Lema, R., Rabellotti, R., & Sampath, P. G. (2018). Innovation Trajectories in Developing Countries: Co-Evolution of Global Value Chains and Innovation Systems. *The European Journal of Development Research, 30*(3), 345–363.

Liao, S., Liu, Z., & Zhang, S. (2018). Technology Innovation Ambidexterity, Business Model Ambidexterity, and Firm Performance in Chinese High-Tech Firms. *Asian Journal of Technology Innovation, 26*(3), 325–345.

Lorenzen, M., & Mudambi, R. (2013). Clusters, Connectivity and Catch-Up: Bollywood and Bangalore in the Global Economy. *Journal of Economic Geography, 13*(3), 501–534.

Lu, Y. (2017). Industry 4.0: A Survey on Technologies, Applications and Open Research Issues. *Journal of Industrial Information Integration, 6*, 1–10.

Makino, S., Lau, C.-M., & Yeh, R. S. (2002). Asset Exploitation Versus Asset-Seeking: Implications for Location Choice of Foreign Direct Investment From Newly Industrialising Economies. *Journal of International Business Studies, 33*(3), 403–421.

Malerba, F. (1992). Learning by Firms and Incremental Technical Change. *The Economic Journal, 102*(413), 845–859.

Mathews, J. A., & Cho, D. (1999). Combinative Capabilities and Organizational Learning in Latecomer Firms: The Case of the Korean Semiconductor Industry. *Journal of World Business, 34*(2), 139–156.

Morrison, A., Pietrobelli, C., & Rabellotti, R. (2008). Global Value Chains and Technological capabilities: A Framework to Study Learning and Innovation in Developing. *Countries Oxford Development Studies, 36*(1), 39–58.

Park, T. Y. (2013). How a Latecomer Succeeded in a Complex Product System Industry: Three Case Studies in the Korean Telecommunications Systems. *Industrial and Corporate Change, 22*(2), 363–396.

Pietrobelli, C., & Startiz, C. (2018). Upgrading, Interactive Learning, and Innovative Systems in Value Chain Interventions. *European Journal of Development Research, 30*(3), 557–574.

Rapoza, K. (2020, April 10) Kudlow: Pay the Moving Costs of American Companies Leaving China. *Forbes.*

Rothaermel, F. T. (2001). Research Note: Incumbent's Advantage Through Exploiting Complementary Assets Via Interfirm Cooperation. *Strategic Management Journal, 22*(6-7), 687–699.

United Nations Conference on Trade and Development (UNCTAD). (2020). *World Investment Report 2020: International Production Beyond the Pandemic.* New York: United Nations.

Ustundag, A., & Cevikcan, E. (2018). *Industry 4.0: Managing the Digital Transformation.* Cham: Springer International.

Velten, J. (2020, August 10). *FDI Screening Regulation and the Recent EU Guidance: What Options Do Member States Have?* Columbia FDI Perspectives No 284.

Witt, M. A. (2019). De-Globalization: Theories, Predictions, and Opportunities for International Business Research. *Journal of International Business Studies, 50*(7), 1053–1077.

Zeng, D. Z. (2010). How Do Special Economic Zones and Industrial Clusters Drive China's Rapid Development? In D. Z. Zeng (Ed.), *Building Engines for Growth and Competitiveness in China: Experience with Special Economic Zones and Industrial Clusters* (pp. 1–53). Washington, DC: International Bank for Reconstruction and Development/World Bank.

Zhou, S., Baskaran, A., Tang, M., & Rasiah, R. (2017). Adaptive Innovation in the Evolution of a Latecomer Firm: The Case of Asiainfo. *Institutions and Economics, 9*(2), 75–108.

CHAPTER 4

Chinese Diplomacy, Strategic Partnerships and Global Economic Supremacy

Maria Papageorgiou and Fabio dos Santos Cardoso

Abstract China's rising potential as a great industrial power has generated widespread interest; however, there has been little attention to the role of its extensive network of strategic partnerships in its power projection. This study investigates the role of China's strategic partnerships in its global rise by borrowing elements of the network model from business studies and by drawing on similarities with a firms' internationalization process.

Keywords Internationalization • Strategic partnerships • Network model • China's rise • Bilateral relations • Economic • Military power

M. Papageorgiou (✉)
University of Minho, Braga, Portugal
e-mail: maria_marypapageorgiou@hotmail.com; id7645@alunos.uminho.pt

F. dos Santos Cardoso
School of Economics and Management, University of Minho,
Braga, Portugal

F. Spigarelli, J. R. McIntyre (eds.), *The New Chinese Dream*,
Palgrave Studies of Internationalization in Emerging Markets,
https://doi.org/10.1007/978-3-030-69812-6_4

4.1 Introduction

China's impressive economic performance in the early 2000s represents a "transformative process" in terms of global political economy (Henderson and Nadvi 2011) but has also raised salient questions on its newly acquired global importance. The country's economic performance has facilitated the modernization of the Chinese army; increased military expenditures as well as China's soft power, supporting China's successful "global externalization". The process of China's 'global externalization' (Henderson and Nadvi 2011) is based on trade, technology, and elements of Chinese culture. China today stands as the world's second-biggest economy while ranking first in terms of purchasing power parity (PPP), value-added manufacturing, merchandise trading, and as the largest foreign exchange reserves holder in the world (Morrison 2019).

An essential element of China's road to becoming a global power has been its "new diplomacy" adopted since the early 1990s to facilitate its economic expansion and promote bilateral diplomatic engagement (Wang 2008). A diplomatic tool that China has employed widely to enhance bilateral cooperation is strategic partnerships. Chinese officials emphasize the importance of partnership diplomacy in the country's external relations (Swaine 2015) particularly. China commenced its first partnership with Brazil in 1993, followed by Russia in 1996. Since then, Beijing has been actively engaged in developing strategic partnerships with several countries expanding its presence in many geographical regions.

China's strategic partnerships share similar characteristics such as high--level official meetings, advanced trade ties and win-win cooperation arrangements (Muekalia 2004). China has concluded 110[1] partnerships with other countries and regional organizations as of 2019 that differ both in name and essence from one another. Each joint statement between Beijing and a partner outlines the areas of cooperation and the mechanisms established to advance the relationship. There have been various designations assigned to each partnership[2] depending on the intensity of

[1] Xi calls for expansion of global partnerships, China Daily, 2019, https://www.chinadaily.com.cn/a/201909/09/WS5d754883a310cf3e3556a5bd.html.

[2] All-weather strategic cooperative partnership, Comprehensive strategic partnership of coordination, All-round strategic partnership, Strategic and cooperative partnership for peace and prosperity, Comprehensive strategic partnership, Strategic cooperative partnership, Strategic partnership. Source: Chinese Ministry of Foreign Affairs, fmprc.gov.cn/mfa_eng/gjhdq_665435/.

cooperation and the "degree of proximity between China and its partners" (Li and Ye 2019, p. 67). The partnerships are also regularly upgraded, showing that "partnership relations usually need time to develop and pass through different stages" (Strüver 2017, p. 43). Overall, these partnerships have proven to be a powerful instrument to guarantee a favorable environment for China's rise (Zhongping and Jing 2014) and elevate its status at the systemic level (Yu 2015). Thus, the country's extensive network of partnerships and categorizations of those partnerships account for a strategic motivation in promoting both its internationalization in economic terms as well as its status as a great power in military and political terms.

This Chapter investigates how network relationships contribute to China's "internationalization" process. By adopting an exploratory research design, we apply the business network model to explain China's quest to be a global power. This approach looks closer to the country's numerous strategic partnerships with other states and analyses them by employing social network analysis. We argue that the business network model is well-suited to explain the behaviour of contemporary great powers in the international arena and provides an understanding of how power is established and promoted. To further support this argument, the authors employ descriptive statistics to collect the data, while network analysis reveals the presence of patterns in different types of relationships (Wasserman and Faust 1994). The graphical display complements the findings and ranks China's top ten partners in distinct dimensions on its partnership network. The selected methodology is not commonly used in International Relations or International Business (Maoz 2012; Kurt and Kurt 2020).

The three areas of cooperation analyzed are military, economic and political with each one divided into two subcategories. Arms transfer and military activities fall under the military dimension. Outward foreign direct investments (OFDI) and trade exports are used to evaluate the economic dimension. Lastly, the voting similarity in the United Nations General Assembly, as well as the presence of Confucius institutes, represent the political dimension. The analysis is longitudinal accounting for a ten year period, starting from 2008 and concluding in 2018 due to data availability. This period was selected to account for China's resilience in the face of the 2008 financial crisis and its subsequent growth referred by the Chinese government as the "New Normal",[3] "a new growth model that relies less on fixed investment and exports, and more on private consumption, services, and innovation to drive economic growth" (Morrison 2019, p. 1). Between 2008 and 2018, MultiTech giants, such as Huawei, Xiaomi, and Alibaba propelled China's economic and technological advancements while the newly introduced economic initiatives such as the BRICS, Asian Infrastructure Investment Bank (AIIB) and the Belt and Road Initiative show that Beijing also seeks to achieve its foreign policy goals (Paradise 2016).

The chapter is structured as follows; the first section bridges the business internationalization process with international relations presenting similarities and selects the network model as the best model to investigate this process. The second section outlines the methodology employed, and in sequence, the empirical analysis follows presenting the findings in a visual format. Lastly, the conclusion summarizes the results of this study which indicate that China's strategic partnerships have been instrumental in advancing China's efforts to shape a favourable environment for its rise.

4.2 Internationalization and the Network Model from Business Studies to International Relations

International relations and business studies share similar characteristics to an extent. Both States and firms seek to achieve goals; firms pursue profit and a bigger share in the market and similarly the objective for states is survival in an anarchical international system. Firms tend to expand their activities by seeking new business opportunities in foreign markets. This is translated to a high degree of internationalization that indicates the establishment of strong links with entities from various countries (Forsgren 1989; Johanson and Mattsson 1988; Turnbull and Valla 1986). These links are materialized in the form of strategic alliances or partnerships. Gulati (1998, p. 619) defines them "as a voluntary agreement between firms involving exchanges, sharing, or co-development of products, technologies, or services".

There are many incentives for firms to form alliances: entering new markets, offering a more complete solution, sharing and reducing risks, accessing new technologies, etc. However, despite the many promising

[3] The previous period which concluded in 2007, was characterized as the "Chinese Miracle", due to the spilled over effects of China's rising global influence see (Naughton 2018).

reasons to partner up, many alliances never achieve success. A study by McKinsey (2007) shows that only 51% of all partnerships achieve returns greater than the cost of capital. Therefore, companies must exercise due diligence before agreeing with any potential partner to check whether specific criteria are fulfilled. Pankaj (2001) and Ricart et al. (2004) identified four sensitivity dimensions that companies consider in the internationalization process: (1) Cultural, (2) Administrative, (3) Geographic, and (4) Economic. This so-called CAGE framework and highlights the importance of other factors such as governmental influence, national interests, and the diversification of business channels in the development of outboard investments. Thus, a decision to cooperate is fundamentally of a strategic intent, which aims at improving the future circumstances for each firm. Consequently, strategic alliances and partnerships play a central role in the establishment and expansion of the network and consequently in the level of a company's internationalization.

For states, from the neorealist viewpoint, the ultimate goal is either survival or a strong position in the international system (Waltz 1979; Mearsheimer 2001). To achieve that, states try to enhance their own military capabilities and establish alliances. However, in the post-Cold War era alliances have declined to a significant extent and a new term gained prominence in the foreign policy discourse of states, strategic partnerships. A strategic partnership refers to a 'special relationship' with both neighbouring and distant countries. Despite the term's frequent use and its widespread appeal, there is no consensus on the definition of the term, while its scope is quite broad (Renard 2010; Mytelka 1991). There are several definitions of how strategic partnerships are to be understood and what they entail in the academic world. Wilkins (2012) considers strategic partnerships as the expression of collaboration between two or more states, in a loose and non-binding way formed to address common challenges in different areas. In the same vein, Bennett and Krebs (1994) emphasize on the common goals of the partnering sides and define the partnership as the cooperation of various actors that are willing to cooperate to reach these goals.

Nevertheless, a decision to cooperate in both business and international relations is not a responsive action, and except its transactional nature, it has a strategic intent, aiming to improve future circumstances for each unit (Vonortas and Zirulia 2015). In business, the goal of a firm, its internationalization which has been studied by developing models such as the Uppsala Model (Johanson and Valne 2009), Global Alliance Model

(Ohmae 1989) and the Network model (Johanson and Mattsson 1988). The network model is defined as "the establishment, development and maintenance of relations between the network participants" (Ratajczak--Mrozek 2012, p. 30).[4] Johanson and Mattsson's (1988) approach was developed to explain how industrial firms develop their internationalization process, focusing on the interdependence among international market, knowledge and trust as cumulative assets. Among the key features is the establishment of long-term relations between business actors based on technical, economic, legal and above all personal ties. Moreover, Carson et al. (2004) indicate how the network linkage's strength is dependent on trust, commitment and cooperation developed between the central node and its partners. Johansson and Mattson's argue that companies are dependent on resources that other firms control, and by holding a position within a network, they can get the right of entry to these resources by creating and maintaining relationships within the networks (Johanson and Mattsson 1988; Johanson and Vahlne 2003).

Drawing on the characteristics defined in Johanson and Mattsson's, the network model (1988), the main argument of this chapter is that China's network of strategic partnerships secures the use of market assets, such as critical resources, information and legitimacy and develops high levels of personal ties and trust between the partnering countries to achieve its own "internationalization", global rise.

4.3 The Network Model

4.3.1 *Methodology*

This interdisciplinary study applies social network analysis (SNA) to elaborate on how networks advance key international outcomes. SNA examines the relationships among social entities, and the implications they have (Wasserman and Faust 1994) while as an analytical tool, that is based on graph theory, enables systematic documentation and representation of relationships (Hanneman and Riddle 2005; Scott 2000). Maoz (2012) underlines that social network analysis can support the understanding of the interactions between different agents (countries or companies) inside a complex system. It also allows us to understand the relations and structures which link one node to another (Falcone et al. 2020).

[4] See also Turnbull and Valla (1986), Johanson and Mattsson (1988, p. 287).

China's numerous strategic partnerships can be portrayed as a network defined as "a finite set or sets of actors and the relation or relations defined on them"(Wasserman and Faust 1994: 20). A specific characteristic of China's partnership network is centrality, highlighting its central position, but also used as an index of the power, prestige and influence that the central node claims in the network (Brass 1984; Sparrowe et al. 2001). In network terms, the nodes refer to the states and the links to the transmission channels in various dimensions between nodes. The strength of the links is indicative of the frequency of interactions between two nodes and the intensity of bilateral cooperation. Since China's strategic partnership network is argued in this study to facilitate its rise as a global power, the notion of power is perceived as the material capabilities of each state (Waltz 1979). Thus, following an operationalization of power based on tangible material capabilities, we investigate China's bilateral relations with its partners under three dimensions military, political and economic that apprehend tangible and intangible components of power. To assess the intensity of cooperation between China and its partners in each dimension, we use descriptive statistics which allows the systemic observation, summarizing and categorizing the data. A graph visualization outlines the results of how the network is composed and the ten most important partners in each subcategory during the period of analysis (2008–2018).

For the military dimension, we include the arms transfers and bilateral military activities with data collected from SIPRI,[5] China's firepower,[6] PLA official webpage[7] and various other sources.[8] The arms transfers are calculated as the volume of arms exported by China to its partners in aggregate numbers (US dollars). The second subcategory of military activities is calculated as the sum of bilateral military exercises, naval port calls and senior-level meetings between PLA and its counterparts from other countries.

In the economic dimension, the two subcategories include the overall trade and outward foreign direct investments. For overall trade, we use the summation of total exports with data extracted from "The Observatory of

[5] Stockholm International Peace Research Institute sipri.org.

[6] globalfirepower.com.

[7] China Military webpage english.chinamil.com.cn.

[8] Annual report to US Congress Military and Security Developments Involving the People's Republic of China 2008–2018, Ministry of National Defence of the People's Republic of China http://eng.mod.gov.cn/news/node_48741.htm.

Economic Complexity", OEC.[9] On the second subcategory, we focus on direct investments calculated in the same manner as trade exports. The investments values were obtained with a sum of the amounts of those sectors: (1) agriculture; (2) chemical; (3) energy; (4) entertainment; (5) finance; (6) health; (7) logistics; (8) metals; (9) real state; (10) technology; (11) transport; (12) utilities; (13) tourism; and small amounts of other economic sectors, represented under the denomination (14) "others". This indicator seeks to identify which are China's strategic destinations and in which sectors. Each sector had its yearly amount of Chinese investment summed in an accumulated value at the end of the period started in 2008 and finished in 2018. China Global Investment Tracker[10] was the source to collect this data.

Lastly, in the political dimension the United Nations General Assembly voting similarity is calculated based on the number of similar votes in the yearly resolutions using data by Voeten's database, UN's digital library.[11] The second subcategory of this dimension included the number of Confucius institutes in each country as of 2018 with the data retrieved from the official Confucius institute headquarters webpage.[12]

4.3.2 *Empirical Analysis*

China's economic, military and political involvement in different continents reflects its desire to create its own sphere of influence and elevate its power status at the world system (Yu 2015). In these three dimensions, China has built distinct networks composed of different partners. The visualization of China's network is presented below (Fig. 4.1), allowing us to observe in more detail the variations in the country's partnership framework.

Military Dimension

Military cooperation can take various forms: equipment procurements, arms transfers, joint military exercises, nuclear disarmament cooperation, transfer of military technology, exchanges of military personnel, joint trainings and development of common doctrines (Schwartz 2019). For

[9] https://oec.world/en/.

[10] https://www.aei.org/china-global-investment-tracker/.

[11] UN Digital gallery https://digitallibrary.un.org/.

[12] Confucius Institute Headquarters english.hanban.org/.

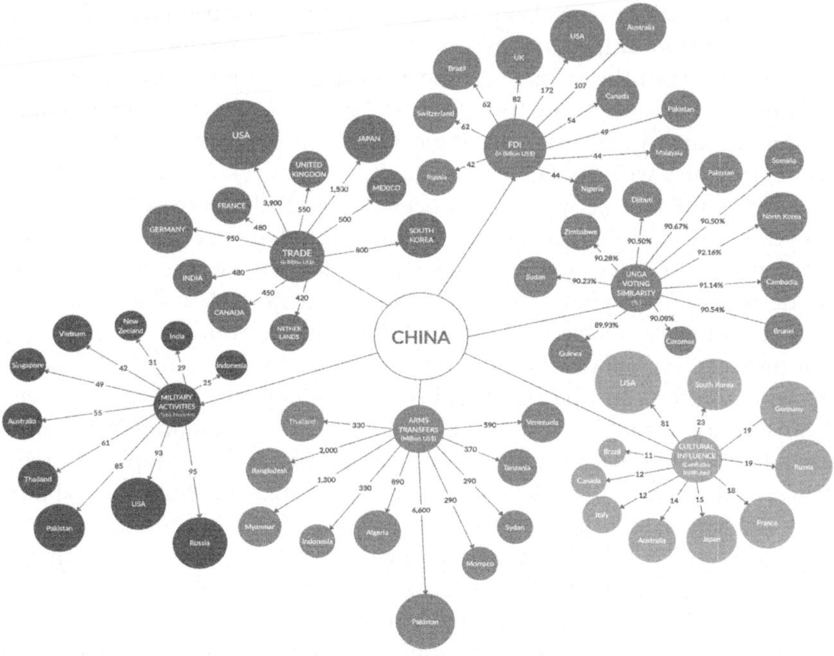

Fig. 4.1 Chinese network of partnerships. (Authors' elaboration)

our analysis, the military dimension is divided into two subcategory arms transfers and military activities to showcase China's growing presence on the military domain. Since 2010 China has expanded its arms exports to new countries is now considered one of the "world's leading arms exporters" (Raska and Bitzinger 2020). According to data from SIPRI in the last ten years, China has been ranked as the fifth and later fourth-largest arms exporter in the world (Wezeman et al. 2018). Most of China's arms exports are sold to developing countries, signalling an increased competition with Western countries and Russia for markets (Raska and Bitzinger 2020).

The results indicate that six countries-Pakistan, Iran, Iraq, North Korea, Myanmar, and Thailand have been China's primary arms transfer recipients. The results show that China has been advanced to an important arms exporter not hesitating selling arms to "pariah" states such as Iran, North Korea, and Myanmar (Raska and Bitzinger 2020; Byman and Clift 1999).

China's arms sales except from the economic perspective have also a strategic dimension enhancing its political influence in regions such as its neighbouring Southeast Asia and the Middle East. A large amount of arms transfers to Pakistan is due to the two countries close relationship characterized as an "All-weather Strategic Cooperative Partnership" and the strategic rivalry with India.

China's military activities have been significantly increased in the last 15 years with President Xi Jinping announcing that they represent a critical element of China's foreign policy.[13] To that end, Beijing has strived to modernize and upgrade its armed forces to defend and promote its regional interests, such as its territorial claims in the South China Sea, keep the pressure on Taiwan not to declare independence and to defend its growing interests around the world by establishing itself as a rising power. China's People's Liberation Army (PLA) has grown significantly since the early 1990s along with the frequency, complexity and geographical orientation of its activities. These activities include military exercises, naval port calls and senior-level meetings conducted in bilateral or multilateral form and also under UN peacekeeping operations and antipiracy activities (Saunders and Shyy 2019). China's first joint military exercise Peace Mission 2005 was conducted alongside Russia under the auspices of Shanghai Cooperation organization in Vladivostok and Weifang and Qingdao between August 18–25, 2005 (Andrew 2005). In the last decade, PLA has also gained an edge over other regional competitors in the Asia--Pacific region, a region that has heavily fall under the U.S.-led alliance system (Liff and Ikenberry 2014).

The analysis indicated that regarding the military activities, China holds close ties with two other great powers USA and Russia, followed by its neighbouring countries. Among the other countries that frequently conduct military activities with China are Australia and four members of ASEAN, Thailand, Vietnam, Singapore and Indonesia, indicating a geographic orientation towards Asia. There has also been a strengthening of cooperation with India and New Zeeland, the last five years. In terms of the specific activities China and Russia conduct joint military exercises more frequently, China and Pakistan hold the highest number of naval port calls, whereas China and the USA have the most senior meetings exchanges. The strong cooperation with Russia and Pakistan showcases

[13] CPC news, January 29, 2015, http://cpc.people.com.cn/n/2015/0129/c64094-26474947.html.

the durability of these bilateral relationships and the wide range of operative activities. Nonetheless, and despite the high level of military activities between China and the USA, their cooperation hinders a strategic competition in South East Asia.

Political Dimension

To examine the political dimension of China's rise, we explore the country's diplomatic cooperation under the UN and its cultural promotion. The Chinese government has invested significantly in language and culture exchange abroad. China's growing cultural power with the promotion of the Chinese language facilitates its "soft power" (Ding and Saunders 2006) similarly to the US promoted cultural initiatives in the aftermath of the second world war (Nye 2004). The establishment of Confucius Institutes back in 2004 is considered to showcase China's goal of peaceful development and desire to share its culture with the world (Paradise 2009) but also its attempts to achieve a more sympathetic global reception (Pan 2013). However, many countries expressed doubts in regards to Confucius institutes' activities describing them as a "Trojan Horse", a vehicle to strengthen China's growing geopolitical influence which endangers other states national security (Kluver 2014).

The results indicate China's cultural network to be geographically focused on Europe (a total of 187) with Germany, France and Italy having the highest number of established institutes. The American continent and Asia follow with 138 and 135 respectively while in Africa there has been a two-fold increase in just the last five years reaching 61 in number. The country with the most Confucius institutes in the world and a significant difference to the second is the USA. Russia is placed in the fourth position while other Asian and neighbouring countries such as Thailand and South Korea followed.

The second subcategory in the political dimension accounts for the voting patterns in the United National General Assembly which constitutes an excellent indication to understand the alignments of states in international politics (Kim and Russett 1996). Moreover, they can pinpoint the formation of voting blocs and the common interests of states (Voeten 2013). The issues discussed in UN general assembly refer to the constant developments in the international arena and indicate similar positions among states. The voting patterns of China's partners showcase whether they share common worldviews and the extent of the country's leadership influence (Strüver 2016).

According to the results, the countries that vote in agreement with China are mostly underdeveloped African countries Djibouti, Zimbabwe, Guinea, Somalia and Sudan. This could be explained by the heavy dependence of these countries on China's humanitarian aid and investments (Strüver 2016). China sees in its African partners' opportunities for energy resources, expansion of trade activities but also geopolitical considerations (Muekalia 2004). Pakistan remains amongst China's closest partners ranked third in this subcategory, with North Korea ranked first and Cambodia second. Besides the top ten ranked partners, the analysis showed that the other countries that have a voting similarity over 88% with China are Cuba, Myanmar, Laos and Iran. It is worth noting here that these countries have a similar political regime to China, therefore making it more likely to lead in policy convergence (Dreher et al. 2018).

Economic Dimension
China has expanded its trade relations with various countries while having sought new markets through its network of partnerships. The country remains the most important exporter in the commodities market, is characterized as "the biggest commodity hub in the world" (Nobi et al. 2020). The Belt and Road Initiative and its ambitious structure are perceived to be an important turn for the country, advancing its role from a commodity trader to a diversified one and an attempt to create a global common trade and investment zone (Chaisse and Matsushita 2018).

The amount of exports, as well as the destination, helps us understand the intensity of the economic relations among the Asiatic Giant and its buyers. The results indicate that China's exports to just its top ten partners reached the amount of over 10 trillion dollars in the ten years of analysis. This shows China efforts to stabilize and expand its economic performance but also to uphold its position in strategic markets, in all regions. The United States imports the most, followed by Japan, Germany and South Korea. Together they, imported around 7.1 trillion dollars. Two other countries of the European Union, France and the United Kingdom are significant importers of Chinese products adding up more 1 trillion dollars. The value of China's yearly exports of goods to the world surpasses the amount it imports, leading to a continuous trade surplus for the country since 1994 (China Power Team 2019). In addition, strong trade links can shape national perceptions as it has been observed in China--Africa relations (Sautman and Hairong 2009).

In the last two decades, China's has been elevated to one of the most important sources of outward foreign direct investment (OFDI) (OECD 2019). The Chinese government has strongly encouraged its leading business firms to engage in investment activities under the context of "globalizing China" (Yeung and Liu 2008). To expand China's presence, a great deal of investments has been directed across all continents. A total of 716 billion dollars was invested abroad during the period of analysis. The results indicate that the top recipients of Chinese investments in the ranking sequence are the United States, Australia, United Kingdom, Brazil, Switzerland, Canada, Pakistan, Malaysia, Nigeria and Russia. The establishment of partnerships has assisted China in alleviating the political risks arising by directing its foreign direct investments in partner countries that have already engaged in favourable agreements and collaborative projects. According to Sun and Liu (2019, p. 131) "the establishment or upgrade of partnerships has a positive impact on Chinese firms' decisions on OFDI."

4.4 Conclusion

This study demonstrates that China's use of strategic partnerships holds similarities to the business network model in promoting its internationalization process by seeking expansion to new markets, acquiring resources, gaining a competitive edge and establishing a favourable image. By focusing on three dimensions economic, military and political, we identified that China has developed a network of partners that differ in areas and intensity of cooperation, and strategic intent.

The results also exhibit that China puts great emphasis on promoting cooperation with its neighbouring countries, also showing a geographical focus towards Asia. Moreover, China's strategic partnerships with Asian countries showcases an attempt to limit US influence in the region, promoting itself as "a credible rival to the United States in the region" (Bitzinger 2011, p. 7). This strategy could be explained by theoretical considerations implying that China seeks to maximize its power in the region and becoming a regional hegemon (Mearsheimer 2010).

The network analysis also helps identify which countries are more dependent on China's trade exports and investments with the USA and European states being in the top positions followed by Asian and African countries indicating the broad reach of the Chinese economic activities. On the military dimension, concerning arms transfers, middle and small power states compose the network. At the same time, in military activities which is interrelated with defence and security issues, the main partners are Russia and Pakistan with the USA also holding a prominent position. In the political dimension and particularly in UN General Assembly voting African countries and long-standing ally North Korea are positioned higher, and the Confucius institutes show a widespread geographical distribution being an imperative feature of China's soft power. To this end, it is important to note that the USA still remains in the top positions in many of the subcategories analyzed, showing that the strong economic and military interdependence between the two could halt China's rising potential.

China's strategic partnerships network has yielded significant achievements in expanding the country's global influence and standing in the international system. In conclusion, strategic partnerships have been employed by China to develop a global network of interconnectivity to uphold and further develop its economic capacity, secure a stable geopolitical environment across its borders, modernize its army, alleviate US pressure in South East Asia and eventually facilitate its global rise.

One aspect that is important to be evaluated in the future is how strong is the formed network and how committed China's partners will be under a growing competition between great powers. Besides, since the term strategic partnership originates in business and organizations studies, further research on China's power and interstate relations could be facilitated under an interdisciplinary approach that accounts for the market dynamics, business ecosystems and the criteria for partner selection.

References

Andrew, M. (2005). Power Politics: China, Russia, and Peace Mission 2005. *China Brief, 5*(20), 8–9.

Bennett, R. J., & Krebs, G. (1994). Local Economic Development Partnerships: An Analysis of Policy Networks in EC-LEDA Local Employment Development Strategies. *Regional Studies, 28*(2), 119–140.

Bitzinger, R. (2011). Modernising China's Military, 1997–2012. *China Perspectives, 2011*(2011/4), 7–15.

Brass, D. J. (1984). Being in the Right Place: A Structural Analysis of Individual Influence in an Organization. *Administrative Science Quarterly*, 518–539.

Byman, D. L., & Clift, R. (1999). *China's Arms Sales Motivations and Implications (No. RAND/MR-1119-AF)*. RAND. Santa Monica.

Carson, D., Gilmore, A., & Rocks, S. (2004). SME Marketing Networking: A Strategic Approach. *Strategic Change, 13*(7), 369–382.

Chaisse, J., & Matsushita, M. (2018). China's Belt and Road Initiative: Mapping the World's Normative and Strategic Implications. *Journal of World Trade, 52*(1), 163–185.

China Power Team. (2019). "Is China the World's Top Trader?" China Power. Centre for Strategic and International Studies. March 28, 2019.

Ding, S., & Saunders, R. A. (2006). Talking Up China: An Analysis of China's Rising Cultural Power and Global Promotion of the Chinese Language. *East Asia, 23*, 3–33. https://doi.org/10.1007/s12140-006-0021-2.

Dreher, A., Fuchs, A., Parks, B., Austin, M. S., & Tierney, M. J. (2018). Apples and Dragon Fruits: The Determinants of Aid and Other Forms of State Financing from China to Africa. *International Studies Quarterly, 62*(1), 182–194.

Falcone, P. M., D'Alisa, G., Germani, A. R., & Morone, P. (2020). When All Seemed Lost. A Social Network Analysis of the Waste-Related Environmental Movement in Campania, Italy. *Political Geography, 77*(102114), 1–17.

Forsgren, M. (1989). *Managing the Internationalisation Process: The Swedish Case.* London: Routledge.

Gulati, R. (1998). Alliances and Networks. *Strategic Management Journal, 19*(4), 293–317.

Hanneman, R. A., & Riddle, M. (2005). *Introduction to Social Network Methods.* Riverside, CA: University of California.

Henderson, J., & Nadvi, K. (2011). Greater China, the Challenges of Global Production Networks and the Dynamics of Transformation. *Global Networks, 11*(3), 285–297.

Johanson, J., & Mattsson, L.G. (1988). Internationalisation in Industrial Systems—A Network Approach. In N. Hood & J.-E. Vahlne (Eds.), *Strategies in Global Competition.* Croom Helm. Reproduced in P. J. Buckley & P. Ghauri (Eds.), The Internationalisation of the Firm: A Reader. New York: Academic Press.

Johanson, J., & Vahlne, J. E. (2003). Business Relationship Learning and Commitment in the Internationalization Process. *Journal of International Entrepreneurship, 1*(1), 83–101.

Johanson, J., & Vahlne, J. E. (2009). The Uppsala Internationalization Process Model Revisited: From Liability of Foreignness to Liability of Outsidership. *Journal of International Business Studies, 40*(9), 1411–1431.

Kim, S., & Russett, B. (1996). The New Politics of Voting Alignments in the United Nations General Assembly. *International Organization, 50*(4), 629–652. https://doi.org/10.1017/S0020818300033531.

Kluver, R. (2014). The Sage as Strategy: Nodes, Networks, and the Quest for Geopolitical Power in the Confucius Institute. *Communication, Culture & Critique, 7*(2), 192–209.

Kurt, Y., & Kurt, M. (2020). Social Network Analysis in International Business Research: An Assessment of the Current State of Play and Future Research Directions. *International Business Review, 29*(2), 101633.

Li, Q., & Ye, M. (2019). China's Emerging Partnership Network: What, Who, Where, When and Why. *International Trade, Politics and Development, 3*(2), 6681. https://doi.org/10.1108/ITPD-05-2019-0004.

Liff, A. P., & Ikenberry, G. J. (2014). Racing Toward Tragedy? China's Rise, Military Competition in the Asia Pacific, and the Security Dilemma. *International Security, 39*(2), 52–91.

Maoz, Z. (2012). How Network Analysis Can Inform the Study of International Relations. *Conflict Management and Peace Science, 29*(3), 247–256.

McKinsey and Company Special Collection. (2007). Report.

Mearsheimer, J. J. (2001). *The Tragedy of Great Power Politics.* WW Norton & Company.

Mearsheimer, J. J. (2010). The Gathering Storm: China's Challenge to US Power in Asia. *The Chinese Journal of International Politics, 3*(4), 381–396.

Morrison, W. M. (2019). *China's Economic Rise: History, Trends, Challenges, and Implications for the United States.* Washington, DC: Congressional Research Service.

Muekalia, D. J. (2004). Africa and China's Strategic Partnership. *African Security Studies, 13*(1), 5–11. https://doi.org/10.1080/10246029.2004.9627264.

Mytelka, L. K. (Ed.). (1991). *Strategic Partnerships: States, Firms, and International Competition.* Associated University Presse.

Naughton, B. J. (2018). *The Chinese Economy: Adaptation and Growth.* MIT Press.

Nobi, A., Lee, T. H., & Lee, J. W. (2020). Structure of Trade Flow Networks for World Commodities. *Physica A: Statistical Mechanics and its Applications, 556*, pp. 124761.

Nye, J. S., Jr. (2004). Soft Power. In *Power in the Global Information Age.* Routledge.

OECD. (2019). Economic Surveys China April 2019 OVERVIEW. http://www.oecd.org/economy/surveys/china-2019-OECD-economic-survey-overview.pdf.

Ohmae, K. (1989). Managing in a Borderless World. *Harvard Business Review, 67*(3), 152–161.

Pan, S. Y. (2013). Asian Education and Development Studies. *Studies, 2*(1), 22–33. https://doi.org/10.1108/20463161311297608.

Pankaj, G. (2001). Distance still matters. *Harvard Business Review (Electronic Journal), 79*(8), 1–12.

Paradise, J. F. (2009). China and International Harmony: The Role of Confucius Institutes in Bolstering Beijing's Soft Power. *Asian Survey, 49*(4), 647–669.

Paradise, J. F. (2016). The Role of 'Parallel Institutions' in China's Growing Participation in Global Economic Governance. *Journal of Chinese Political Science, 21*(2), 149–175. https://doi.org/10.1007/s11366-016-9401-7.

Raska, M., & Bitzinger, R. A. (2020). Strategic Contours of China's Arms Transfers. *Strategic Studies Quarterly, 14*(1), 91–116.

Ratajczak-Mrozek, M. (2012). The Network Model of Internationalisation. In K. Fonfara (Ed.), *The Development of Business Networks in the Company Internationalisation Process*. Poznań: Poznań University of Economics Press.

Renard, T. (2010). Strategy Wanted: The European Union and Strategic Partnerships. *Security Policy Brief, 13*(4) Retrieved from http://aei.pitt.edu/15061/1/SPB13-EU-Strategic-Partnerships.pdf.

Ricart, J. E., Enright, M. J., Ghemawat, P., Hart, S. L., & Khanna, T. (2004). New Frontiers in International Strategy. *Journal of International Business Studies, 35*(3), 175–200.

Saunders, P. C., & Shyy, J. (2019). *China's Military Diplomacy in 'China's Global Influence': Perspectives and Recommendations*. Edited by S. D. McDonald & M. C. Burgoyne. Asia-Pacific Center for Security Centre.

Sautman, B., & Hairong, Y. (2009). African Perspectives on China-Africa Links. *The China Quarterly, 199*, 728–759.

Schwartz, P. N. (2019). The Military Dimension in Sino-Russian Relations. In *Sino-Russian Relations in the 21st Century* (pp. 87–111). Cham: Palgrave Macmillan.

Scott, J. (2000). *Social Network Analysis: A Handbook* (2nd ed.). London: Sage.

Sparrowe, R. T., Liden, R. C., Wayne, S. J., & Kraimer, M. L. (2001). Social Networks and the Performance of Individuals and Groups. *Academy of Management Journal, 44*(2), 316–325.

Strüver, G. (2016). What Friends are Made of: Bilateral Linkages and Domestic Drivers of Foreign Policy Alignment with China. *Foreign Policy Analysis, 12*(2), 170–191.

Strüver, G. (2017). China's Partnership Diplomacy: International Alignment Based on Interests or Ideology. *The Chinese Journal of International Politics, 10*(1), 31–65.

Sun, C., & Liu, Y. (2019). Can China's Diplomatic Partnership Strategy Benefit Outward Foreign Direct Investment? *China & World Economy, 27*(5), 108–134.

Swaine, M. D. (2015). Xi Jinping's Address to the Central Conference on Work Relating to Foreign Affairs: Assessing and Advancing Major-Power Diplomacy with Chinese Characteristics. *China Leadership Monitor, 46*(1), 10–11.

Turnbull, P. W., & Valla, J. P. (1986). Strategic Planning in Industrial Marketing: An Interaction Approach. *European Journal of Marketing, 20*(7), 5–20.

Voeten, E. (2013). *Data and Analyses of Voting in the UN General Assembly*. Routledge Handbook of International Organization, ed. B. Reinalda (Published May 27, 2013). Retrieved from http://ssrn.com/abstract=2111149.

Vonortas, N., & Zirulia, L. (2015). Strategic Technology Alliances and Networks. *Economics of Innovation and New Technology, 24*(5), 490–509.

Waltz, K. (1979). *Theory of International Relations*. Reading, MA: Addison-Webley.

Wang, Y. (2008). Analyzing Feature in China's New Diplomacy: Strategic Dialogues and Multilateral Diplomacy. In P. Kerr, S. Harris, & Q. Yaqing (Eds.), *China's 'New' Diplomacy: Tactical or Fundamental Change*. Basingstoke, UK: Palgrave Macmillan.

Wasserman, S., & Faust, K. (1994). *Social Network Analysis: Methods and Applications*. Cambridge: Cambridge University Press. https://doi.org/10.1017/CBO9780511815478.

Wezeman, P. D., Fleurant, A., Kuimova, A., Tian, N., & Wezeman, S. T. (2018). *Trends in International Arms Transfers*. SIPRI.

Wilkins, T. S. (2012). Alignment', Not 'Alliance'–The Shifting Paradigm of International Security Cooperation: Toward a Conceptual Taxonomy of Alignment. *Review of International Studies, 38*(1), 53–76.

Yeung, H. W. C., & Liu, W. (2008). Globalizing China: The Rise of Mainland Firms in the Global Economy. *Eurasian Geography and Economics, 49*(1), 57–86.

Yu, L. (2015). China's Strategic Partnership with Latin America: A Fulcrum in China's Rise. *International Affairs, 91*(5), 1047–1068. https://doi.org/10.1111/1468-2346.12397.

Zhongping, F., & Jing, H. (2014, June 27). *China's Strategic Partnership Diplomacy*. ESPO Working Paper No. 8. https://doi.org/10.2139/ssrn.2459948.

CHAPTER 5

Is China Going to Run the Digital World?

Dominique Jolly

Abstract The chapter addresses the digital landscape in China. China has succeeded over the past twenty years in articulating and implementing a strategic vision of a powerful national system of innovation. This system has begun to yield significant technological results in the digital transformation fields. The contribution also lists various reasons as to the dramatic growth of digital fields inside China-including protectionism precluding US companies from penetrating the Chinese market, and the resulting preponderant influence of China due to its enormous population. Several examples of future possible application domains, such as driverless cars and smart cities, are considered. It must be recognized that China has been able to run its own digital world, responding to its innovatory and

Thanks to: Claude Chaudet (Webster University Geneva), Georges Haour (IMD), Olivier Linossier (Olilab), Bruce McKern (UTS Business School), Lennart Rudstrom (Bikmis), and Liqiong Shen (BNP Paribas) for their very useful comments on draft versions of this chapter.

D. Jolly (✉)
Webster University Geneva, Geneva, Switzerland
e-mail: jolly@webster.ch

F. Spigarelli, J. R. McIntyre (eds.), *The New Chinese Dream*, Palgrave Studies of Internationalization in Emerging Markets, https://doi.org/10.1007/978-3-030-69812-6_5

entrepreneurial growth needs. Important impediments to the development of Chinese digital potential externally are discussed in the final section.

Keywords Digital industry • Chinese innovation • Protectionism • Trade war

5.1 Introduction

This chapter argues that China has succeeded over the past 20 years in strategically developing and implementing a powerful national system of innovation, and that this system has begun to produce significant technological results in the digital field. The chapter also lists several reasons why the digital economy has dramatically developed inside China—including protectionism precluding US companies to enter the Chinese market, and preponderant influence of China due to its enormous population. Several examples of future possible application domains, such as driverless cars and smart cities can all be developed within the country. As a matter of fact, China has been able to run its own digital world. However, several important impediments to the development of the Chinese digital potential externally are discussed in the final section.

5.2 A Solid Eco-System which Fostered Digital Technology Creation

All possible external means were developed in the past to obtain technological knowledge developed outside China: joint-ventures, licensing contracts, purchase of equipment, takeovers, spying, etc. But, the more recent reality in the past few decades is that technological innovation has been developed inside China (Haour and Jolly 2014; Fu 2015; Haour and von Zedtwitz 2016; Yip and McKern 2016). This is because the country has strategically assembled together all the essential ingredients for a productive "National System of Innovation" (Nelson 1993): large innovative companies, science and technology parks, start-ups, unicorns, universities and public research centers. Since 2019, China has spent more per annum for R&D than the USA (if you apply purchasing power parity rates).

Financing has not been an issue; different levels of government—central, provincial, or municipal, have provided generous funding to companies, numerous private equity funds have been set-up, and venture capitalists are very active. On the top of this, foreign companies have setup over 1500 R&D centers (Jolly et al. 2015). A brief survey of the system of innovation in the digital area brings this home.

5.2.1 Big Innovative Companies

On the hardware side, Huawei is well known for its smartphones. But it received international recognition in the (B2B) telecom equipment industry, thereby accomplishing an impressive journey (Tian and Wu 2015). The company started in Shenzhen in 1987 as a supplier of telephone equipment, targeting small towns and rural areas in China. Then, after a decade of growth, the firm launched an international strategy in 1997. In 2004, Huawei was only 1/6 the size of Ericsson, the global leader at that time. By targeting easy-to-reach countries, Huawei built a significant market base. In 2010, Huawei became the world number two in telephone equipment behind Ericsson. Then, it gradually extended into developed countries. It now supplies leading operators in Europe like Orange, Vodafone, British Telecom, Deutsche Telecoms and Telefonica. Since 2017, Huawei has obtained the largest share of the global infrastructure market. It invests considerable sums in R&D with a work force of more than 50,000. In 2019, Huawei became the first patent applicant in the world. Its total revenue exceeds 100 billion dollars.

In the (B2C) telecom handset industry, several major players have emerged—including Huawei, Xiaomi, ZTE, Lenovo, Gionee, Meizu, Honor, and Vivo. Xiaomi has made the most impressive route. Created from scratch in 2010, it now sells more than 100 million phones yearly; its success lies in a combination of entrepreneurship, keeping abreast of the evolving market, R&D investment, continuous technological improvement, outsourcing of production, distribution on the web, and diversification in connected products. Its market value went up to 60 billion dollars, but declined to 50 in 2019. Yet, Huawei has still the largest market share in the Chinese market.

On the soft side, the Chinese internet has fostered the development of companies which reached the firmament of stock-market valuation. This includes the well-known BAT trio—Baidu, Alibaba, and Tencent. Alibaba started with B2B, Tencent with gaming, and Baidu with a search engine.

But all are now digital eco-systems through the combination of R&D, infrastructures, service platforms, and content production. Applications cover a large range: B2B, B2C, C2C, messaging, social networks, retail banking, fund management, mobile payment, music streaming, video streaming, mapping, Cloud, etc. Tencent was ranked 18th in the "2013 World Most Innovative Companies" by Forbes magazine, and the company is the twelfth of the Top 50 of the "Most Innovative Companies 2015" of the BCG. But the Chinese internet is also constituted by major distribution companies such as Jindong, Pinduoduo, and Yihaodian, which are threatening the traditional brick and mortar distributors. In addition, the Chinese internet developed in many directions: microblogging with Weibo, taxi reservation with Didi, video sharing with Bytedance and Tiktok, tourism with Ctrip, and meal delivery with Meituan. Chinese firms are also very active in the financial technology (fintech) sector. Chinese companies have led the *Fintech 100* for several years with three in the top 10 in 2019 and many start-ups in the top 100. The top 10 include Ant Financial, JD Digits and Du Xiaoman Financial.

Most of those companies are private. Yet in the telecom services, the state controls a highly concentrated oligopoly over three giant telecom companies: China Mobile, China Telecom, and China Unicom. The Herfindahl index is close to 0.50. The biggest, China Mobile, has almost one billion subscribers.

5.2.2 *World-Class Scientific and Technology Parks*

A large part of Chinese success lies in infrastructures. This is also true for technology creation. In 2010, the country had 100 science and technology parks (Jolly and Zhu 2012). This number went to 169 in 2020. They are concentrated in three major regions: Beijing, Shanghai and the Yangzi delta, and Shenzhen and Guangzhou (in the South). Shenzhen is the most exemplary case (it went from a rural county to a megalopolis in 30 years). But Beijing Zhongguancun Science Park, Shanghai Zhangjiang Hi-tech Park, and Suzhou Industrial Park (SIP) are also foremost examples. Zhongguancun is a focal point for chemistry, pharmacy and semiconductor. Zhangjiang is known in information technology, space and biotechnology. Baidu, the Chinese Internet search engine that overwhelmingly dominates the Chinese market is headquartered in Zhongguancun in Beijing.

5.2.3 *A Myriad of Start-Ups, and a Lot of Unicorns*

China is grounding its innovation process also on start-ups. There are many examples: ZhongAn, internet-based property insurance, Qufenqi, an electronics retailer with consumer finance, Lufax, peer-to-peer lending and trading of financial assets, and WeCash, internet credit assessment. Several Chinese firms have emerged as serious actors in artificial intelligence (McKinsey 2017a, April). This includes dedicated start-ups like iFlyTech, Sense Time, Hikvision, and Megvii. iFlyTech is in vocal interfaces. Sense Time, Yitu Technology and Malong Technology are major players in computer vision covering facial, object and image recognition. Megvii (with its flagship software Face ++), created in Beijing in 2011, was valued at $ 4 billion at the end of 2019. All have double-digit R&D to revenue ratios. Many Internet companies have also embarked on the adventure of artificial intelligence: Didi in ride-sharing, Meituan in the meal delivery (as earlier stated), Toutiao in the news aggregation, Metian in selfie beautification, Kuai Shou in the live broadcast or even Deep-Blue in driverless buses. Even drone maker DJI uses artificial intelligence. Interestingly, large companies such as Alibaba and Tencent are used to tap into this reservoir of innovative knowledge to nurture their own technological bases, in China but also abroad.

5.2.4 *Universities and Public Research Centers*

Deeply imbedded Confucianism roots give true respect for education and learning. A cult of intensely competitive performance in schools across the country is exemplified by the high ranking of students in Shanghai, Beijing and the provinces of Jiangsu and Zhejiang as measured by the Pisa ranking (Program for International Students Assessment) from the OECD. About 8 million young Chinese get the Gaokao (high-school diploma) each year. On a total of 30 million university students (vs. 20 million in Europe), China produces 7 million university graduates per year. Notably, in recent years, there has been a change of emphasis towards economics and management with basic sciences attracting fewer students. China is also the largest provider of foreign exchange students in the world (a stock of one million including 350,000 in the USA) and a very large proportion of doctoral students in the USA are Chinese. Those returning graduates contribute to the intellectual dynamism of Chinese universities and public research centers.

The Chinese Academy of Science and the research institutes under the control of ministries play a central role. Chinese scientific research output has developed considerably in the past two decades. Chinese academic entities produced a meager 20.000 articles yearly in 1998. In 2019, 450,000 peer-reviewed articles were published which puts China ahead of the USA. Most of the Chinese universities are teaching universities; they still need to develop a culture of true inquisitive research. Yet, universities such as Tsinghua, Peking, Fudan, Hefei, Zhejiang, Jiaotong, Nanjing and Sun Yat-sen are keen competitors at the international level.

5.2.5 *Booming Patenting Activity*

In 2000, China applied for 50,000 patents; the European Union, for 100,000; Japan, for 400,000, and the USA for 300,000. Now, the tide has turned. China's patent application has dramatically outpaced the USA. In 2018, almost 1.5 million patents were filed and 346,000 granted in China (according to WIPO n.d.). Such a production of innovations was supported by a Chinese regulatory framework inspired from the rules and regulations of Western countries. Interestingly, much of the litigation occurs between Chinese companies. Despite criticism on the value of those patents, the trend is positive. And, in 2019, China surpassed the USA as the top source of international patent applications filled with WIPO (April 7, 2020 Bulletin).

5.3 How Has China Developed a Strong Digital Economy?

With all the actors and the technological resources described in the previous section, China has founded its own powerful digital ecosystem (McKinsey 2017b, August; Kim and Chen 2018). How can the economic success derived from this technology base be explained? Four explanations can be suggested: (a) Chinese companies favored leapfrogging, (b) the Chinese government adopted protectionist measures to foster the development of local champions, (c) China was able to exploit its size advantage, and (d) Chinese companies are in a better position to understand their market than foreign companies. Nevertheless, our conclusion is that China is still dependent on external suppliers.

5.3.1 *Leapfrogging in Emerging Industries*

In 1978, China lagged behind in technology in almost all areas. The few Chinese citizens who traveled abroad before 1978 (including Deng Xiaoping) had been able to grasp the dramatic underdevelopment of their country. Following the South Korea model (Kim 1997), China's strategy has been first to ensure upgrades in activities with low technical content, then to gradually increase in technological sophistication (see Chap. 3). While catching up was the target, overtaking foreigners in several technological fields was unthinkable, especially in mature industries. Yet the situation has been different in emerging industries. In this regard, the Internet seems to be a playground where Chinese companies such as Tencent, for example, are more competitive, at least in their local market.

China skipped the home computer stage; it immediately embraced the smartphone. And the smartphone has invaded the lives of Chinese people much more than it has conquered the lives of Westerners. That is certainly the case with the Wechat application (Weixin in Chinese), launched in 2011 by Tencent. Since 2018, Wechat exceeds 1 billion monthly active users and Tencent exceeds $ 500 billion in capitalization. It is now the norm in communications, for both private and professional use. In less than 10 years, we saw the social network universe pairing with an ecommerce universe to provide a unique interface. While Wechat is a social network that offers the Wechat Pay payment method, conversely, Alipay is a payment platform that has also spread into social networks. Both solutions are now ubiquitous and even necessary in everyday life in China. The use of smartphones has become widespread to pay bills and expenses, to pay for the metro, for ordering and paying at restaurants, for listening to music or watching a video, for ordering a taxi, for paying groceries, for paying for coffee at Starbucks, to rent a bike, to pay the rent, to send a "red envelope" during the holidays,...

The next technological leap ahead of the West might potentially be accomplished with the connected car, in which China is investing heavily: its development will benefit from its market size, and it relies on a particularly vibrant information technology ecosystem which now exists.

5.3.2 *Protectionism*

China was denied the market economy status by the WTO in 2001, a decision that was supposed to be lifted before the end of 2016 (i.e. fifteen years after the accession). But in 2017, the European Union and the USA refused to give to China the market economy status on the grounds that China did not carry out the reforms originally promised in 2001. As a matter of fact, the Chinese State today still very much interferes in the choices of companies. The market is notoriously absent from the financing of state enterprises by (state-owned) banks. Thus, Beijing cannot align itself with the classic liberal model: its banking system would implode. To counter this image, President Xi Jinping came to Davos in 2017, promoting globalization and championing economic free trade—but this posturing does not mean that China is a market economy.

China's digital economy falls clearly in this perspective. The fixation of local norms, the barriers to entry to foreign companies, and especially the Western Tech giant (the so called GAFA), are demonstrations of protectionism. This has helped the Chinese government plan to foster the development of local champions, and to control its cyber sovereignty.

5.3.3 *Size Effect: Huge Network Externalities*

China's first strength is strength in numbers. China has surpassed 800 million Internet users—97% of whom use mobile. These size effects are an extraordinary engine for development. The point is obvious in the telecommunications and the Internet businesses: firms can put several hundred engineers on a given R&D project, while competitors in small countries cannot. In addition, digital tools develop in a specific language—and even if pronunciations vary from one place to another, Chinese writing is the same for 1.39 billion people. The same goes for infrastructure equipment: by 2014, the Chinese had built many more base stations and erected 4G masts than the whole of Europe. Today, its 5G equipment has already been rolled out. In addition, with nearly a billion cell phone subscribers (they were less than 100 million in 2000), China is sure to have an impact on future formats and standards.

5.3.4 *Offerings Fitted with Local Demand*

The Chinese people are far from being uniform. The notion of Chinese people all dressing identically is an image of the past. There are several 'Chinas'. The city and the countryside are two different worlds; idem for smaller towns and larger cities. Differences are also manifest between the north and the south, or between coastal provinces and inland provinces. In product development and the marketing of services, geographical segmentation is the minimum required. Haier, for example, developed a washing machine for inland farmers that washes potatoes as well as clothes. Segmentation is also needed to deal with income dispersion: there are the middle class, the rich, the super-rich and even the ultra-rich. The market dynamics and the strong penetration of the Internet have played a full role in the emergence of these segments. In the telephone sector, for example, it is possible to market, as ZTE has done, a telephone dedicated to the elderly (with large keys and a large screen) or even a telephone dedicated to rural environments—or conversely, a telephone whose use is reserved for a specific city. Chinese companies are much more prepared to deal with those marketing challenges than their foreign counterparts.

5.3.5 *China Is Still Dependent on External Suppliers*

China is so famous for exporting that we forget that it imports too. An overwhelming share of semiconductors consumed in China are purchased in the USA, South Korea and Malaysia, among others. While China accounts for 55% of world demand, 95% of its needs are met by imports—which will exceed $300 billion in 2020 (more than oil imports). China has for decades sought to shake off its reliance on the West for semiconductors (see Chap. 8). Neither acceptable methods (joint ventures, business takeovers, etc.) nor less honorable ones (espionage, intellectual property theft, etc.) have been sufficient so far. This dependence was exemplified by the case of ZTE, which the United States threatened in 2018 of no longer supplying components and which consequently raised questions about its very survival. ZTE could have sunk, but chose to pay a fine to suspend the sanctions. It is because of this weakness that the Chinese government has ambitious investment plans to increase local production of semiconductors. One of the Chinese players is Tsinghua Unigroup—majority-owned by Tsinghua Holdings (100% owned by Tsinghua University) and 49% by a private group (Beijing Jiankun Investment). Tsinghua Unigroup has committed tens of billions of dollars for the buyout of foreign manufacturers (including Integrated Silicon Solutions); however, it failed to take over US giant Micron Technology.

Dependency also exists for software applications—especially for the operating system. Huawei, and all Chinese competitors, use the Google Android operating system. Yet the threat of an American refusal to continue supplying Huawei would have serious consequences. The company internally has a substitute for Android, with the Hongmeng platform, and with Harmony, an evolution of Android. Launching its own operating system is a project which Nokia, BlackBerry, Microsoft, Intel, Palm, Firefox, Samsung and Jolla, have all failed. Even if Huawei succeeds, it would be a major handicap outside of China: apps would work correctly, but the main issue for consumers would be the impossibility to use the Google app store.

The Chinese government is aware of this dependency. This is why one of the two major objectives of the latest (# 14) five-year plan (2021–2025) is precisely technological autonomy. And the country has been working quietly on a highly ambitious project, Made in China 2025, which intends to make China far more self-reliant, while also transforming its industrial technology base (see Chap. 1). Yet it is not yet certain to succeed in all domains of its aspirations.

5.4 Future Digital Applications: Dealing with China Macro-Imbalances

The versatility of digital technologies opens many avenues for future applications. China undertook several projects: driverless cars, smart cities, elderlies, public health, e-yuan, and productivity improvements.

5.4.1 Driverless Cars

The Chinese government wants to take advantage of the emergence of autonomous vehicles—whether they are private cars, taxis, buses, or even trucks. These new concepts can help reduce urban traffic congestion caused by the booming Chinese automobile market, and the resulting air pollution. Given its size, China could become the world's largest market. The relative novelty of the automobile, road infrastructure, and industry in China makes it easier to cope with the blurring of competitive boundaries between car manufacturers, transportation companies, and mass data mining platforms. China is trying to set up, with its national companies, the ecosystem required by autonomous vehicles: manufacturers of sensors, radars and cameras, platform developers, software designers, cartographers, storage companies, integrators, but also investors, lawyers, etc. On the other hand, the weakness of the Chinese in semiconductors will work against the country if the driverless car is to develop.

5.4.2 *Smart Cities*

The technological leap mentioned in the third section is now spreading all around. Smart cities provide a real time interface to service infrastructures including mobility infrastructure as service platforms (autonomous cars, shared transportation,...). This is a huge market for the Internet of Things (IoT) and Artificial Intelligence. And again, it is going to be a means to deal with one of China's major societal challenges, i.e. to reduce pollution.

5.4.3 *Taking Care of the Elderly*

China's major demographic challenge is its aging population (see Chap. 6). At the end of 2014, China had 212.4 million people aged 60 or over, 15.5% of its total population. At the end of 2016, the figure rose to 231 million (16.7%). In 2018, 249 million Chinese were over 60 years old (17%). By 2050, the figure could reach 330 million (24%). A society is considered to be aging when the proportion over 60 years old exceeds 10%. The trend remains the same even if we change the threshold. In a Confucian culture, it is understood that children take care of their parents when they get older. Yet, they will not be able to assume the challenge. Solutions can be found with big data and with the Internet of Things. As such, these seniors represent a huge market.

5.4.4 *Public Health and Big Data*

The challenges for public health are massive. Ninety-nine percent of Chinese citizens have basic health insurance, yet the rights are very limited, especially in the countryside. The situation is even more difficult for migrant workers (170 million people) who are largely excluded from these mechanisms as soon as they leave their place of residence. We are very far from the Hu Jintao social harmony. While OECD countries (rich countries) spend on average 22% of their GDP (in 2013) on social spending (pensions, social assistance and health), China spends only 9%. There are 1.5 doctors per thousand inhabitants in China versus 2.4 in the United States, 3.2 in France and even 4 in Switzerland.

Technology can be a solution and the Covid-19 crisis gives an illustration (see Chap. 1). A striking feature of the Chinese economy is its ability to implement faster than Western companies, and its spontaneous acceptance of new technologies. Adoption goes faster. There is far less reluctance than in the Western world to Big brother issues. When the Covid-19 crisis emerged, an application was developed to identify, localize and track sick patients. Everyone adopted the system where individuals generate QR codes on their mobile phones. Consequently, hospitals worked faster and at a lower cost.

Another aspect is that reaction to events is quicker than in the West. When entrepreneurs see an opportunity, they seize it immediately (Petti and Ederer 2012). One explanation is that decision processes occur faster. When the Covid-19 crisis emerged, it took only a decision from the BYD CEO to redirect some of the factories of its group to the production of medical masks.

5.4.5 *A Digital Currency Controlled by the State: The e-RMB*

China officially launched the e-RMB in September 2020 as a test in different cities (including Xiong'an, Chengdu, Shenzhen, Suzhou). It should be expanded step-by-step to cover all China. The e-RMB is an answer to the rise of cryptocurrencies (such as the Bitcoin) and their underlying principle of decentralisation. Yet, it is not a cryptocurrency, but a digital currency. The e-RMB was developed by the People's Bank of China (PBOC) which owns most of the technology—it issued 130 patent applications related to cryptocurrency ranging from issuance, to circulation, and applications that supports its development. The e-RMB requires users to download an electronic wallet application authorized by the PBOC and to link it to their bank accounts. Users can then pay their bills, get some cash, or execute money transfers. Chinese commercial banks will convert some of their central bank deposits into this digital currency. The money from the linked bank account would be converted into digital cash on a one-to-one basis. China has taken the so called "two-tier" approach making sure their commercial banks are key in the ecosystem (as banks also invest in the infrastructure). The e-RMB currency is a substitute to cash in

China; it should not replace cash, but be a complement. One of the key differences from the private wallets (Alipay, WeChat pay) is that the e-RMB can be used in offline mode. It is a block-chain under the control of the Central bank. The main arguments in favour are its cost effectiveness, efficiency and risk control. In comparison to paper cash and coins, the digital yuan reduces transaction, operational, and maintenance costs. The Chinese government will be able to trace all cash flows, seize accounts, shut down accounts if necessary and the control will be strictly limited to the Central bank. As such, it should help anti-money laundering policies and reduce illicit uses. China wants to accumulate the experience as a forerunner. PBOC wants to include cross-border payments within e-commerce with other countries. This could be closely related to the commercial war with USA and the global currency competition.

5.4.6 Productivity Improvement in Manufacturing

China suffers from weak productivity. Industrial processes mobilize armies of people. Factory tours show several hundred people all, obediently and rhythmically, performing the same sequence of a few handfuls of seconds, repeated throughout the day. Productivity in the USA, Europe or Japan—calculated as the ratio of the GDP to the number of hours worked in the country, is far higher than in China. Many state enterprises and heavy industries are even in decline due to their low productivity.

Despite the sharp rise in costs and the associated erosion of competitive advantage, the Chinese government is not abandoning the manufacturing domain, as evidenced by the national plan published in 2015 entitled "Made in China 2025" noted above. The goal of the project is to move China from a labor-intensive manufacturing economy to more high-tech and, above all, more efficient industrial and service activities. This is to avoid falling into the trap of "middle-income economies" by infusing more advanced technologies. Modernization of the industry gives priority to innovation, restructuring, upscaling and internationalization. China wants to free itself from its dependence on foreign companies. This is to encourage the emergence of national champions in ten industries with high technological content—such as cars using alternatives to the gasoline engine. Could this be the revival of the well-known Maoist slogan "Rely on our own strength?" The traditional suppliers of machine tools—Germany and Switzerland in particular—should still find their account there.

5.5 Issues Raised by China Ruling the Digital World

The digital economy has already boosted the Chinese economy. Will it allow the country not to fall into the middle-income trap, i.e. to bypass the limit of a GDP of 10,000 dollars per capita? Will it allow the country to develop its exportation of digital services? Doubtful? China developed a system well fitted to China. But, the advantage gained from a population of 1.39 billion people sharing the same writing system turns to a competitive disadvantage when it comes to exportation. The emergence of China as a major actor in the digital economy raises several societal issues that could impede its international development in the future. Three limits can be identified: (a) the closed door to foreign companies, (b) the culture of control and censorship, and (c) the criticism of the social credit put in place in China.

5.5.1 *The Door Is Not Open to Foreign Companies*

Economic relations between China and abroad are often marked by the absence of reciprocity. If an imbalance could be conceived at the start of China's economic renaissance, there is no question today that China is the second economic power in the world. The Chinese authorities are preserving their domestic market for the benefit of national champions, by closing public markets or through significant subsidies. This will not help to open doors outside China.

5.5.2 *Internet Control, and Censorship*

Chinese leaders want to control their country's cyberspace. If cybercontrol remained measured until the beginning of the 2000s when the number of Chinese Internet users did not exceed a hundred million, it has been reinforced since 2006 when the number of Internet users increased. Control of the Internet is in the hands of the Central Directorate of Internet Security and Computerization. The mission of this group is to maintain China's "cyber-sovereignty". The principle of the Great Firewall or the Great Wall of the Internet is simple: no content deemed subversive on the Internet and therefore no access to foreign sites liable to disseminate unwanted information. The government fears the dissemination of political ideas deemed sensitive and not Chinese (like Western democracy). We are far from freedom of expression. As everyone knows, Facebook, YouTube, Twitter, Instagram, Pinterest or Snapchat are not accessible; however, all of these platforms have Chinese counterparts. Likewise, the websites of Bloomberg, The Economist, Reuters, The Wall Street Journal and The New York Times are blocked. The Chinese people are also banned from surfing Wordpress sites and even Slide Share.

Censorship is thus in full play on an Internet under surveillance. Since the success of micro-blogging sites like Sina Weibo (an equivalent of Twitter which has hundreds of millions of users), the authorities practice cleaning of messages and do not hesitate to delete the accounts of bloggers who are a little too critical. One of the most commented decisions (outside of China) was the 2016 closure of the Weibo account of Ren Zhiqiang, a retired Beijing real estate developer (Party member) known for his criticism of the government and his 37 million followers. He said that the Xinhua Agency or CCTV should be the voice of the public (who pays for their salaries) and not the voice of the Chinese Communist Party as Xi Jinping argues. He was suspended from the CCP for one year for "publishing false views" contrary to key Party principles; the authorities felt that he had lost the spirit of the Party.

Censorship is well established in the country. Does it go beyond the borders of China? Concerned with preserving their economic interests, politicians and business people carefully avoid discussing touchy matters relating to the nature and practices of the Chinese regime. Human rights, press rights, and the situation of minorities often take a back seat when foreign politicians visit China to sign contracts. Nevertheless, the development of platforms like TikTok is a vector of dissemination of Chinese values: after TikTok censored the video of a young woman who explained all the harm she thought of the treatment of Uighurs, the question arose regarding the company's censorship of the content of certain videos. When China exports its technologies, it exports as well its own values—are we prepared for this? The freedom to do business with China often takes precedence over freedom of expression. Unless the globalization of Chinese companies like Huawei, ZTE or Tencent encourages more transparency.

In the same vein, the control of Uighurs populations using facial recognition software and artificial intelligence received a lot of criticism from the West. Observers can understand the fight against extremism, but raise serious ethical questions at the same time.

5.5.3 *The Social Credit System Frightens the West*

The "social credit" project was announced in 2014 by the Chinese government. It forecasted the possible applications of the Internet of Things, the richness of big data and the power of artificial intelligence. This is the modern version of the individual file kept in the past by the managers of "danwei" (work units guaranteeing work for life, housing, care, retirement, etc.). The system is under the supervision of the NDRC and the Central Bank. It measures the reputation of each of the Chinese citizens through a score based on their driving behavior, the time they take to pay their bills, their defaults, and the use they make of social networks. The system is based on data collected on the Internet, but also on facial recognition systems coupled with camera networks deployed in the country. Each Chinese citizen starts with a capital of 1000 points; and, depending on their actions, they can lose or win. Criticism of the Chinese president on a social media loses points—same for cases of indiscipline at work or unpaid bills. The Chinese citizens who erode their social capital run the risk of being sanctioned: suspension of access to a social network, ban on staying in 4 or 5 star hotels, restriction of transport (by train or by plane), ban on leaving of the territory, prevention of entry to university, prohibition of enrolling children in expensive private schools, refusal of access to credit, prohibition of access to certain positions in state enterprises or certain professions, prohibition to receive state subsidies, to receive honorary titles, etc. The system is in the test phase (notably in Hangzhou, Beijing and Shandong); it is now operational.

5.6 Conclusion

Digital China seems to be not soluble with the Western digital sphere. The most likely scenario for the future will be the competition between the two universes: the presently powerful GAFA on one side, BATX on the other side. The competitive advantage of the Chinese authoritarian government is its planned economy mechanisms, and its definitive control over the Chinese digital stakeholders; this governance framework produced a symbiotic partnership. But exportation will be hard.

China has nevertheless opened a door to exportation of all those new technologies through the Belt & Road Initiative (BRI); the new silk road is not only on earth and on the sea, this is also a digital road fostering connectivity (as seen in Chap. 1). Telecommunications networks, internet connections, the Beidou satellite navigation system (the Chinese GPS), cloud computing, fiber optic cables, IoT, railways digital infrastructures, logistic automation, enterprise resources planning are applications desired by all countries on the new silk roads. There are also plans to establish science parks in several of those countries.

References

Fu, X. (2015). *China's Path to Innovation*. Cambridge, UK: Cambridge University Press.

Haour, G., & Jolly, D. (2014). China: The Next Innovation Hot Spot for the World. *The Journal of Business Strategy, 35*((1), 2–8.

Haour, G., & von Zedtwitz, M. (2016). *Created in China: How China Is Becoming a Global Innovator*. Bloomsbury.

Jolly, D., & Zhu, F. (2012). Chinese S&T Parks: A News Model Is Emerging. *The Journal of Business Strategy, 33*(5), 4–13.

Jolly, D., McKern, B., & Yip, G. S. (2015). The Next Innovation Opportunity in China. Multinationals are Shifting Their R&D Focus from Cost Savings to Knowledge-based Research. *Strategy+Business*, Issue 80, 16–19.

Kim, L. (1997). *Imitation to Innovation: The Dynamics of Korea's Technological Learning*. Boston, MA: Harvard Business School Press.

Kim, Y.-C., & Chen, P.-C. (2018). *The Digitization of Business in China*. Palgrave Macmillan Asian Business Series.

McKinsey Global Institute. (2017a, April). *Artificial Intelligence: Implications for China*. Discussion Paper.

McKinsey Global Institute. (2017b, August). *China's Digital Economy. A Leading Global Force*. Discussion Paper.

Nelson, R. R. (Ed.). (1993). *National Innovation Systems: A Comparative Analysis*. Oxford University Press.

Petti, C., & Ederer, M. (2012). *Technological Entrepreneurship in China: How Does It Work?* Edward Elgar Publishing.

Tian, T., & Wu, C. (2015). *The Huawei Story*. Sage Publications.

WIPO (World Intellectual Property Organization). (n.d.). Statistical Country Profiles. Retrieved from https://www.wipo.int/ipstats/en/statistics/country_zprofile/.

Yip, G. S., & Mckern, B. (2016). *China's Next Strategic Advantage: From Imitation to Innovation*. Cambridge, MA: The MIT Press.

CHAPTER 6

Leapfrogging: The Life Science Sector

Dominique Lepore and Nuoya Chen

Abstract The chapter investigates new trends in the life science sector in China. The chapter first discusses how the Chinese government is promoting innovation and competitiveness for the life-science sector, both to satisfy internal demand and to compete at the international level. Technological progress is then addressed through the prism of the synergetic result of government, academia, private business and capital working together. The life-science sector in China bears the potential to become a world leading industry even if R&D remains a challenge.

Keywords Life science sector • Healthcare industry • R&D

This project has received funding from the European Union's Horizon 2020 research and innovation programme under the Marie Skłodowska-Curie – ITN Industrial Doctorate, Grant agreement No. 766139 This paper reflects only the author's view and the REA is not responsible for any use that may be made of the information it contains.

D. Lepore
Department of Law, University of Macerata, Macerata, Italy
e-mail: d.lepore@unimc.it

F. Spigarelli, J. R. McIntyre (eds.), *The New Chinese Dream*, Palgrave Studies of Internationalization in Emerging Markets,
https://doi.org/10.1007/978-3-030-69812-6_6

6.1 Introduction

The life science sector is one of the most interesting cases to analyse the impact of Chinese selective industrial policies to promote structural economic and social changes. Life sciences are a wide field of study which examine living organisms, including microorganisms, plants, animals, and human beings. The life science sector provides solutions that directly impact on the quality and standard of life with applications in the health domain. It involves companies specialized in biotechnology, pharmaceuticals, biomedical technologies, life systems technologies, nutraceuticals, cosmeceuticals, food processing, environmental, biomedical devices. In the age of big data and Artificial Intelligence (AI), the life-science sector in China, namely the biopharmaceutical and medical related tech companies, are increasingly data focused. Mundane tasks have been automated. The development of new drugs has become much faster and cost effective (Deloitte 2020).

In the last twenty years, China has made huge and rapid progress in this field due to reforms of the supply, increasing support of R&D and investments in technologies for the organization and delivery of services.

Advanced technologies as the Internet of Things (IoT), based on objects communicating with one another through the Internet (Whitmore et al. 2014) is revolutionizing the Chinese healthcare system that still has to cope with ageing of the population and rising number of patients with chronic diseases.[1] In particular, the integration of the IoT in healthcare as the Internet of Healthcare Things (IoHT) with AI and machine learning can enable more time and cost-effective delivery of healthcare (World Economic Forum and Boston Consulting Group 2017).

The life science sector in China, including all companies that are related to human healthcare such as pharmaceutical, genomics, medical device manufacturing, medical resources distribution/management and digital healthcare, is capturing these technological advances.

[1] With an aging population, the Chinese healthcare system is under additional pressure. Life expectancy at birth has reached 76.3 years and the age dependency ratio/old is projected to reach 25% by 2030 and 44% by 2050 (World Bank 2018). Further, chronic diseases have become a leading cause of death, reaching to 86.6% in 2012 (National Health and Family Planning Commission 2015).

N. Chen (✉)
Marie Curie Fellow HEART-ITN Project, University of Macerata, Macerata, Italy
e-mail: cny0824@gmail.com

Such technological trend is shaped by strong governmental policies, rising adoption of personalized healthcare models and sustainable development goals.

The recent outbreak of Covid-19 is somehow considered a "wild card" (Rockfellow 1994) in accelerating the pace of digital healthcare utilization while continuing to spark debates at the international level.

While the U.S. still leads in the many sub sector of the life-science industry, China is catching up. Chinese start-ups are developing algorithms and patents by attracting talents and supporting private sector development with abundant capital, a trained workforce, a complete supply chain and a booming market. However, the US trade war and new regulations to control Foreign Direct Investments (FDI) have recently slowed down international trade and investments in the industry.

The chapter is organized as follows. After presenting how the demand for healthcare has led to more data-driven approaches in life science, the chapter describes the main governmental policies supporting the sector. Then, the international positioning of the industry is discussed, also considering the impact of Covid-19. Lastly, the chapter pictures the topic of smart cities as an interesting area of development for life science, even if viewed with skepticism by the US.

6.2 The Demand for Data-Driven Business Models in the Life Science Sector

The Chinese healthcare system is more complex than that of many other countries due to its large population and regional diversity. The country has a three-tiered system for healthcare delivery. Primary health-care facilities provide affordable first-contact care, while secondary and tertiary care facilities offer specialist referral services (Wu et al. 2019).

Hospitals are overcrowded since most medical resources, such as qualified doctors and advanced medical devices can only be found in tertiary level hospitals (National Health Commission 2018). Thus, patients often experience long waiting times and complain about the treatment and diagnosis process (Lim 2014). There are also noticeable territorial differences in healthcare quality: different provinces operate independently to provide healthcare, with healthcare quality higher in coastal areas and big cities, while lagging in inland regions (EIU 2016).

These circumstances have incentivized the introduction of smart health solutions. The emerging solutions cover the whole health continuum, including healthy living, prevention, diagnosis, treatment and home care stages.

China is advancing in technological development by encouraging tech companies to partner with hospitals for developing innovative infrastructures and new business models in healthcare. For instance, Alihealth, one of the largest smart health business in the Chinese market, partnered with hospitals to improve diagnosis accuracy (Alihealth 2019). Moreover, the company with its online-offline medication and service sale has shown a year-on-year growth for the 2018/2019 financial year of 296.8% and 275.5% respectively (Alihealth 2019).

In this scenario, the Internet of Healthcare Things (IoHT) can support the integration of a value-based care delivery by providing data on key health indicators. This system is based on three principles: (a) systematic measurement of the health outcomes that matter to patients and of the costs required to deliver those outcomes across the full cycle of care; (b) identification of clearly defined population segments and the specific health outcomes and costs associated with those segments; (c) development of customized segment-specific interventions to improve value for each population segment (World Economic Forum and Boston Consulting Group 2017).

Therefore, IoHT together with AI and machine learning techniques are shaping the landscape of the life science sector in China. The transformation of the industry towards data-driven models is raising expectations in delivering time and cost-effective healthcare services and products.

6.3 The Supportive Government Policies

China's central government plays a leading role in the ecosystem of the healthcare sector through its regulatory guidance and financial support. Healthcare reforms are emphasizing the role of the life science industry, which has become the touchstone of technological innovation and international debate. Based on the support from the government and the scientific community, rapid progress in important fields of life science in China has occurred, ranging from genomics and neuroscience to drug and vaccine development (Chen et al. 2007).

Even if initially the health system was not acknowledged for its impact on social and economic development (Meng et al. 2019), there has been a significant shift with the reforms of 2009, namely the Healthy China 2020 plan, which started to address access and affordability in healthcare (Yip et al. 2019).

The main breakthrough of the life science sector is Healthy China 2030 (HC 2030), the long-term national healthcare strategy of 2016. The 'Healthy China 2030' Initiative, along with the '*Guidelines on promoting the healthy and orderly development of the Internet of Things*', and the 'Guidance over the development of the Internet + Healthcare Industry' suggests an emphasis on integrating AI, machine learning and the IoT with the healthcare industry.

HC 2030 promotes public health and disease prevention, shifting from a diagnosis and treatment focused healthcare model to a prevention-based model (CPC Central Committee and State Council 2016). The initiative signals the intention to continue investing in key areas of life science such as precision medicine. The HC 2030 strategy also expands the realm of health innovation beyond economic development through its integration with ecology, implementing the country's commitment to the sustainable development goals (SDGs) (Tan et al. 2018). This relationship is expected to boost the development of biotechnology (O'Toole and Paoli 2017).

Moreover, innovation has been the core focus of the 13th Five-Year Plan (2016–2020). The plan considers the development of the life science sector in synergy with that of the IoT sector, which can accelerate synthetic biology and regenerative medicine techniques with a focus on the development of the biotech industry (State Council 2016).

The specific aims of the HC 2030 are to facilitate the adoption of electronic health records, telemedicine, genomics and other biotechnologies and create demonstrations of network-based biotech applications. These objectives further stimulate capital inflow for large-scale development of personalized medicine treatment, new drugs, bio-breeding and other generation biotech products and services. Further, when considering the development of high-performance medical equipment, the plan stresses the intention to develop medical devices that make use of distinctive strengths of Traditional Chinese Medicine (TCM). The action plan for a Healthy China of the 13-FYP specifically promotes the application of big data in healthcare, driving the development of life science, which will become more data-driven.

In this area, China has been making remarkable progress in establishing the necessary digital infrastructure, including digital health records and care management systems, and regional and national level health data sharing platforms (World Bank and DRC 2019).

Above all, life science is a key component of the industrial plan Made in China 2025 (MiC2025), which is seeking to engineer a shift in China's position as a low-end manufacturer to a high-end producer of goods. The plan targets high-technology fields, such as the pharmaceutical industry, which is currently dominated by the developed economies, in an attempt to move China's economy up the value-added chain. The policy guidance document stresses the importance of producing more self-developed drugs rather than manufacturing generic drugs. The plan aims to register in Europe and the U.S. 10–20 innovative therapies and chemical products and develop 5–6 international brands in the medical device sector such as Mindray. To support the success of such a strategy, the policy stresses the importance of government-coordinated efforts in technology standardization, marketization and the nationalization of core technologies (State Council 2015).

In a complementary way, the New Generation Artificial Intelligence Development Plan (AIDP), released in 2017, has the goal of making China the world leader in AI by 2030. The AIDP stresses the development of both smart medical and smart health/aging solutions. The AIDP promulgates the development of medical robotics, smart diagnostic assistant based on image recognition. Regarding pharmaceutical R&D, the plan points to the direction of genome recognition, proteomics, metabolomics based on AI. The plan also promotes smart pharmaceutical regulation and strengthens epidemic intelligence monitoring, prevention and control (State Council 2017).

Meanwhile, the national health commission has replaced the multiple organizations supervising and directing the healthcare system for resource allocation, authentication and standardization. The current national health commission covers functions ranging from the management of the aging population and of health education, to pharmaceutical standardization and policymaking and disease prevention (National Health Commission 2020). While insufficient intellectual property rights protection in China is still a major concern for many pharmaceutical companies, over the years China has devoted considerable efforts to bring its patent practice in line with accepted international standards (Lu et al. 2015).

Another critical area under scrutiny is medical ethics and data management. In this regard, the AIDP outlines its intention to define ethical norms and standards, even if efforts to do so are at the initial stage. In the meantime, government affiliated bodies and private companies in AI practices have been developing their own AI ethics principles (Knight 2019).

6.4 The Chinese Life Science Sector and the Global Exposure

Based on an increasing healthcare demand, technological capabilities and favourable policies, analysed in the previous paragraphs, China is set to become a crucial player in the life sciences as a global leader in drug discovery and innovation.

China is the second largest pharmaceutical market globally, second to the US, with USD 137 billion in total spending in 2018 (IQVIA 2019). The market size for pharmaceuticals is projected to reach USD 161.8 billion by 2023 (Sina Finance 2019). By 2030, the size of the market device in China is expected to be more than 25 percent share of the world's medical device industry at over US$200 billion, second again to the US, who is projected to cross US$300 billion in sales in the same period (KPMG 2018). Even with the decline in the first quarter of 2020 for pharmaceutical sales, the prospects for the Chinese innovation in the pharmaceutical industry is worth expectation given the huge investment in the sector (Jiangkangke 2020).

Moreover, the biotechnology sector has become one of the key drivers for economic growth, forecasting to account for 4% of GDP in 2020. The number of biological science research parks is also growing (Arranz 2018) as well as International collaboration in the life-science sector. In 2019 Wuxi Municipality and Wuxi High-tech District alongside Astra Zeneca opened a life sciences park and a start-up incubator to attract global firms in the healthcare system (Xinhua 2019).

As a result, the life-science and healthcare industries in China have witnessed a transformation from a weak group of inward-looking domestic companies into a group of aggressive players with a global impact, serving as vital links in the global life science supply chain (KPMG 2013).

The life-science sector continues to be an area of interest for foreign investments. In 2014, a new circular allowed foreign investors to hold a 100 percent ownership of hospitals.[2] In 2019, the development of "new raw material for the production of vaccines" and the establishment of "medical institutions" were added to the 2019 National Encouraged List

[2] Notice on Launching Pilot Programmes of Establishment of Wholly-Foreign Owned Hospitals (Ref. Guo Wei Yi Han (2014) No. 244) (the "2014 Notice"), 关于开展设立外资独资医院试点工作的通知, available at: http://www.mofcom.gov.cn/article/b/f/201408/20140800711993.shtml.

for Foreign Investments. Therefore, foreign investors manufacturing raw materials for the production of vaccines and cell-therapy drugs and those investing in medical institutions services can access preferential treatment, such as tax incentives, simplified procedures or discounted land prices. Although, it must be noted that foreign investment in medical institutions is still limited to joint venture structure and cooperation with Chinese companies, unless special approval has been granted (Asia Briefing 2020).

Furthermore, the U.S.-China technology cold war continues to threaten technology advancement in the life-science sector. On the U.S. side, since October 2018, the Committee on Foreign Investment (CFIUS) has strengthened the administrative review of acquisitions and investments for foreign investment in "sensitive sectors" with "critical technologies". Investment projects in the biotech and pharmaceutical industries are under strict scrutiny, especially from China. Before 2018, the U.S. was the top destination outbound investment for Chinese Life Science and Health Care (LSHC) companies (Deloitte 2017).

On the Chinese side, between 2012 and 2016, the Chinese LSHC industry received USD12.35 billion of foreign investments (Deloitte 2017, 2020). The US was ranked in the first position for overseas investment targets of Chinese LSHC companies, far ahead of other countries by both the number and value of investment projects. However, China M&A activities in LSHC have slowed down in 2019 with a decrease of 24% in total deal count and value. As shown in the Fig. 6.1, the total count of deals has reduced in particular for biopharma.

The intensified trade frictions between the US and China (as anticipated in Chaps. 1 and 2) have been affecting the confidence of investors and so has the new EU framework for the screening of FDI of the 10th of April 2019.[3] Even if this framework is aimed at safeguarding Europe's security and public order and does not specifically target China, it created a more complex procedural context for the specific categories of investments involved.

[3] Regulation (EU) 2019/452 of the European Parliament and of the Council of 19 March 2019 establishing a framework for the screening of foreign direct investments into the Union.

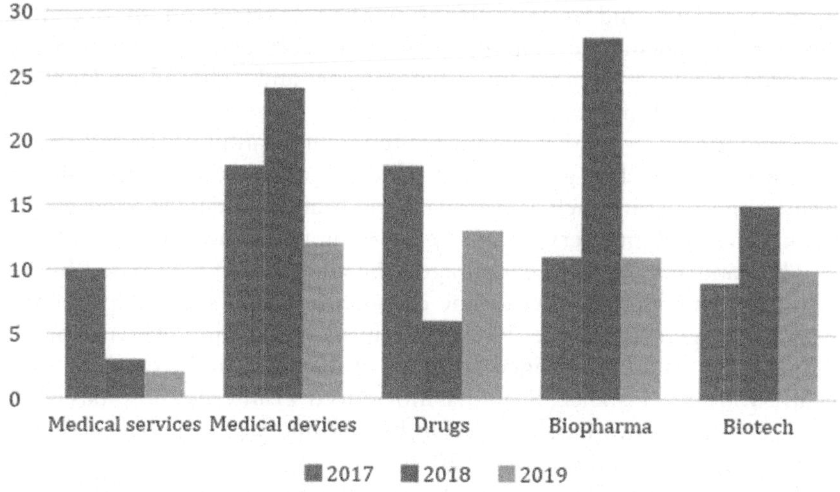

Fig. 6.1 Cross border deal volume by target sector in China. Source: Authors' elaboration based on the research conducted by Deloitte (2020)

6.5 The Wild Card of COVID-19 and Its Effects on the Life Science Industry

The Covid-19 pandemic can be pictured as a "wild card", namely an event that had a low probability of occurring but an extremely high impact (Rockfellow 1994). The life-science is unavoidably the sector where pandemic will have long-lasting implications.

Admittedly, the pandemic facilitated and accelerated the digitalization of the healthcare industry and the use of AI in diagnosis, treatment and health monitoring and management. On the other hand, the pandemic will continue to slow down the treatment of patients with non-urgent chronic diseases such as cardiovascular diseases (Blecker et al. 2021).

During the pandemic, the Chinese government rapidly organized large-scale testing, treatment and prevention measures to control the spread of the disease. Meanwhile, tax reliefs were offered as part of the fiscal stimulus packages for the life-science sector.[4] The Chinese govern-

[4] Tax update on China's pharma & healthcare sector after COVID-19 available at: https://www2.deloitte.com/cn/en/pages/life-sciences-and-healthcare/articles/covid19-impact-on-china-lshc-industry-tax-update.html.

ment, academia and manufacturers worked in coalition in decoding genomic sequencing, developing diagnosis kits, screening potential drugs, conducting clinical research, publishing policies and technical guidance on clinical trials and medical reviews (PWC 2020).

Covid-19 has created a catalyst for the digitalization of the healthcare system in China. The government refocuses on building critical digital health infrastructure such as national wide healthcare data sharing framework, offering digital services, and promoting public health.

The pandemic has also encouraged the adoption of web based hospitals. Internet hospitals offer online consultation, online prescription and health management services based on remote monitoring. The use of AI, 5G, and big data has changed the pace of diagnosis and treatment (Sun et al. 2020). For instance, Shanghai introduced 11 internet hospitals while MedTech businesses reacted quickly by shifting many of their activities online (McKinsey and Company 2020).

Therefore, the Covid-19 is accelerating the transformation of the treatment and diagnosis-based healthcare model to a prevention-based healthcare model. The vast amounts of medical data collected, and new digital diagnostic tools used, and online consultation platforms built during the Covid-19 are optimizing the quality of diagnosis, treatment and prevention (Wong 2020). Though telemedicine is not a new concept in China, the government has only recently started to adopt a more cohesive and regulated approach to this subsector.

Additionally, while in the past the medical devices and equipment approval and regulation procedures were more stringent, a gradual uptick of fast-track registration and ease in approval requirements is emerging (Asia Briefing 2020). Furthermore, environmentally friendly medical innovations complying with SDGs are expected to define the future directions for biotechnology (Hoffman 2020).

All the trends mentioned, ranging from technological advances, favourable policies, patient-led models and SDGs may find a future development in the theme of smart cities, as the last paragraph will discuss.

6.6 Technology, Health Care and Smart Cities: A Novel Scenario to Consider

The advantage and potential benefits to use technology to provide medical support in daily routine as well as in emergency situations, has been proven during the time of the pandemic. The Covid 19 outbreak has set the ground for a further push towards the organization and governance of cities with a massive use of technology, and data driven services. The future seems more and more oriented toward the governance and organization of smart and technological cites, i.e., high-tech advanced city that are able to connect people, information and urban services through technologies creating a sustainable, greener, and innovative environment for residents (Bakici et al. 2013). Smart cities can collect data from multiple sources, including mobile device, sensor data and different service networks such as transportation, healthcare and energy supply (Cook et al. 2018) and improve the way data is retrieved, processed, stored and disseminated for detecting and containing outbreaks, such as Covid-19 (Costa et al. 2020). Moreover, smart cities can support urban planning and infrastructure construction efficiency, providing waste management at a lower cost (Mehmood et al. 2017). Other possible areas of application are in the fields of population surveillance, active ageing, healthy lifestyles and response to emergencies (Rocha et al. 2019).

Smart city development projects are already driving massive transformations in the life science sector. Major trends include increasing demand for preventive and personalized healthcare and the need for governments to make high quality healthcare accessible to citizens, as already mentioned in the previous paragraphs (Muhammed et al. 2018).

Also, the pharmaceutical industry, comprising complex procedures, functions and organizations involved in developing and manufacturing drugs and medical products could benefit from smart cities logistics. For instance, by integrating the IoT within smart cities it is possible to enhance the accuracy, integrity, and security of products and services provided, ensuring that the incoming raw materials, processing, and outgoing drugs and equipment are critically examined before being dispatched from the production warehouse (Jain and Sharma 2020). Moreover, biotechnology can be applied in smart cities in synergies with the IoT sector, finding application in green smart cities concepts (Gotovtsev and Dyakov 2016) in line with the SDGs.

Some of the leading technology companies in China are already working on smart city initiatives alongside the municipalities. An interesting case is that of Ping An, which is one of the major financial groups in China, working on developing online medical insurance refund systems as well as online health consultation and management platforms. The company has announced the launch of a platform "1+N", at the Fourth China Smart City International Expo 2018 in Shenzhen. The platform integrates and supports different smart city sectors including not only healthcare, elderly care, environmental protection but also smart government, civil affairs, finance, security, transportation, ports and education. The smart cities technologies could thus favour connectivity between different sectors (Ping An 2020; Xinhua Newsnet 2020).

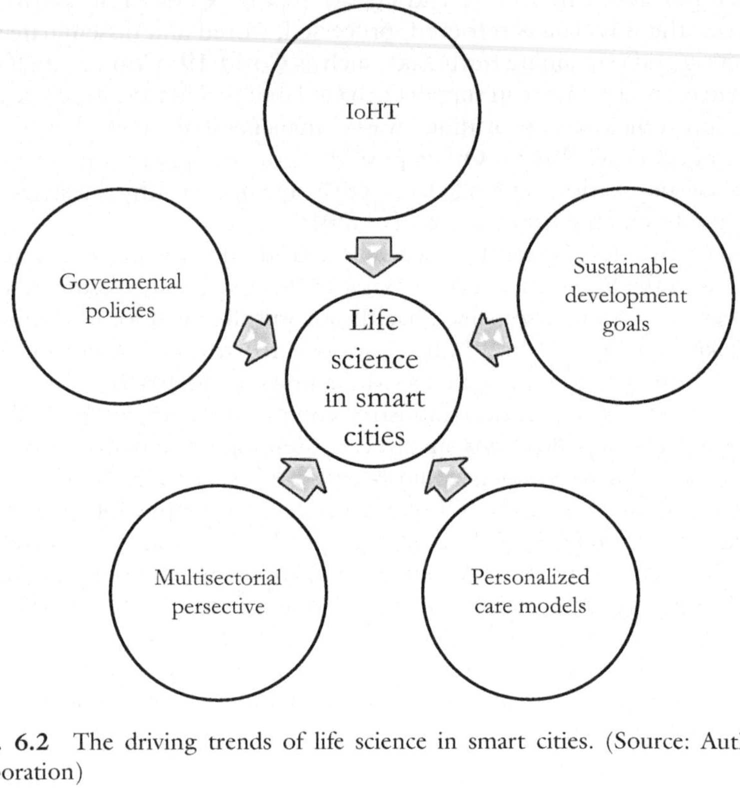

Fig. 6.2 The driving trends of life science in smart cities. (Source: Authors' elaboration)

Overall, the Covid-19 has accelerated the trends that are shaping the development of the life science sector, as presented in the Fig. 6.2.

However, even if remote diagnosis and medicine enhanced by smart cities could facilitate information sharing and improve personalized care, special care must be given to guarantee privacy and property of personal data, especially because smart cities spread all over the world and emerge with similar features and interdependencies at the global level (Dameri et al. 2019). Since February 2020, China has speeded up the international promotion of some of its smart city technologies in international markets, as disinfecting robots, drones and AI and Cloud services (Ekman and Picardo 2020). Through these avenues, the growth of Chinese smart cities exports presents a serious economic and security challenge to the US (Atha et al. 2020).

6.7 Conclusions

The life science industry in China has the potential to become a driver for the country's economic growth. Current policies such as HC2030 and Made in China 2025 are supporting the integration of personalized care models and IoHT. The sustainable development goals are also shaping the development of the life science sector. These trends can be exploited in the novel scenario of smart cities, in which the country has been already investing before the Covid-19 pandemic.

Nevertheless, several countries have tightened FDI screening mechanisms, establishing new regulations or are planning such steps, to protect their health sector and other industries that they consider as particularly important in the Covid-19 crisis. The European Commission introduced a new communication reinforcing FDI screening, based on the premise that the Covid-19 emergency could increase risks by acquiring healthcare capabilities and research establishments through FDI (European Commission 2020a, 2020b). Moreover, the pandemic has resurfaced debate on the ethical and legal boundaries of deploying digital tools for public health.

Therefore, though progress has been made in critical infrastructure and hardware manufacturing, the potential for developing a life science industry with strong international competitiveness is yet to realize in China (BGI Ventures 2020). Initiatives to support long-term growth and innovation in healthcare delivery and life science are likely to be a core part of the 14th FYP (2021–2025).

References

Alihealth. (2019). *Annual Report 2018/19*. Retrieved September 14, 2019, from http://doc.irasia.com/listco/hk/alihealth/annual/2019/ar2019.pdf.

Arranz, A. (2018, October 9). Betting Big on Biotech. *South China Morning Post*. Retrieved from https://multimedia.scmp.com/news/china/article/2167415/china-2025-biotech/index.html.

Asia Briefing. (2020). *Opportunities for Foreign Investors in China's Service Industries After COVID-19*. Dezan Shira & Associates.

Atha, K., Callahan, J., Chen, J., Drun, J., Francis, E., Green, K., et al. (2020, January). *China's Smart Cities Development*, Research Report Prepared on Behalf of the U.S.-China Economic and Security Review Commission.

Bakici, T., Almirall, E., & Wareham, J. (2013). A Smart City Initiative: The Case of Barcelona. *Journal of the Knowledge Economy, 4*, 135–148.

Blecker, S., Jones, S. A., Petrilli, C. M., Admon, A. J., Weerahandi, H., Francois, F., & Horwitz, L. I. (2021). Hospitalizations for Chronic Disease and Acute Conditions in the Time of COVID-19. *JAMA Internal Medicine, 181*(2), 269. https://doi.org/10.1001/jamainternmed.2020.3978.

Chen, Z., Wang, H.-G., Wen, Z.-J., & Wang, Y. (2007). Life Sciences and Biotechnology in China. *Philosophical transactions of the Royal Society of London. Series B, 362*, 947–957.

Cook, D. J., Duncan, G., Sprint, G., & Fritz, R. (2018). Using Smart City Technology to Make Healthcare Smarter. *Proceeding of IEEE, 106*(4), 708–722.

Costa, D. G., Paolo, J., & Peixolo, J. (2020). COVID-19 Pandemic: A Review of Smart Cities Initiatives to Face New Outbreaks. *IET Smart Cities, 2*, 64–73.

CPC Central Committee and State Council. (2016). Outline of 'Healthy China 2030' Plan [in Chinese].

Dameri, R. P., Benevolo, C., Veglianti, E., & Li, Y. (2019). Understanding Smart Cities as a Glocal Strategy: A Comparison between Italy and China. *Technological Forecasting and Social Change, 142*, 26–41.

Deloitte. (2017). China Life Sciences and Health Care Investment Promotion Report.

Deloitte. (2020). 2020 China Life Sciences and Health Care M&A Trends Report. Retrieved from https://www2.deloitte.com/content/dam/Deloitte/cn/Documents/life-sciences-health-care/deloitte-cn-pr-lshc-ma-trends-en-200428.pdf.

EIU. (2016). China's Healthcare Challenges: The People's Hospital of Yiyang County in Henan Province: A Case Study from the Economist Intelligence Unit. Retrieved January 31, 2019, from http://vbhcglobalassessment.eiu.com/wp-content/uploads/sites/27/2016/10/EIU_Medtronic_CaseStudy_Chinas_Healthcare_Challenges.pdf.

Ekman, A., & Picardo, C. (2020, May). *Towards Urban Decoupling. China's Smart City Ambitions at the Time of Covid-19*. European Union Institute for Security Studies, Brief.

European Commission. (2020a). EU Foreign Investment Screening Regulation Enters into Force. Retrieved October 23, 2020, from https://ec.europa.eu/commission/presscorner/detail/en/IP_19_2088.

European Commission. (2020b). *Communication from the Commission*. Guidance to the Member States Concerning Foreign Direct Investment and Free Movement of Capital from Third Countries, and the Protection of Europe's Strategic Assets, Ahead of the Application of Regulation (EU) 2019/452 (FDI) Screening Regulation.

Gotovtsev, P. M., & Dyakov, A. V. (2016). *Biotechnology and Internet of Things for Green Smart City Application*. 2016 IEEE 3rd World Forum on Internet of Things (WF-IoT), Reston, VA, 542–546.

Hoffman, A. (2020). The Post-Pandemic Planet: Will Our Relationship with the Natural World Really Change?, World Economic Forum. Retrieved from https://www.weforum.org/agenda/2020/06/planet-pandemic-environment-nature-coronavirus-covid19/.

IQVIA. (2019). *The Global Use of Medicine in 2019 and Outlook to 2023*. Forecast and Areas to Watch.

Jain, A., & Sharma, D. K. (2020). Chapter 3: Transforming Pharma Logistics with the Internet of Things, *An Industrial IoT Approach for Pharmaceutical Industry Growth*, 2, 55–85.

Jiangkangke. (2020). Negative Market Size Growth for the Pharmaceutical Industry in China. Retrieved October 21, 2020, from https://www.cn-healthcare.com/article/20200813/content-540874.html.

Knight, W. (2019). Why does Beijing suddenly care about AI ethics? MIT Technology Review. https://www.technologyreview.com/s/613610/why-does-chinasuddenly-care-about-ai-ethics-and-privacy/.

KPMG. (2013). *Healthcare & Life Sciences in China. Towards Growing Collaboration*. A Report.

KPMG. (2018). Medical devices 2030. https://assets.kpmg/content/dam/kpmg/xx/pdf/2017/12/medical-devices-2030.pdf.

Lim, J. (2014). WeChat Is Being Trialled To Make Hospitals More Efficient In China. *Forbes*. https://www.forbes.com/sites/jlim/2014/06/16/wechat-isbeing-trialed-to-make-hospitals-more-efficient-in-china/#660828d855e2,%20accessed%20on%20Sep%2016th%202019.

Lu, M., Bai, S., Tan, Y., & Xu, C. (2015). Pharmaceutical Intellectual Property Rights in China. In M. Lu (Ed.), *Approaching China's Pharmaceutical Market*. Cham: Springer.

McKinsey & Company. (2020). How COVID-19 Is Reshaping China's Medtech Industry.

Mehmood, Y., Ahmad, F., Yaqoob, I., Adnane, A., Imran, M., & Guzani, S. (2017). Internet-of-Things-Based Smart Cities: Recent Advances and Challenges. *IEEE Communications Magazine, 55*(9), 16–24.

Meng, Q., Mills, A., Wang, L., & Han, Q. (2019). What Can We Learn from China's Health System Reform? *BMJ, 365*.

Muhammed, T., Mehmood, R., Albeshri, A., & Katib, I. (2018). UbeHealth: A Personalized Ubiquitous Cloud and Edge-Enabled Networked Healthcare System for Smart Cities. *IEEE Access, 6*, 32258–33228.

National Health and Family Planning Commission of the People's Republic of China. (2015, June 30). Report of National Nutrition and Chronic Disease Status.

National Health Commission. (2018). Health System Review 2017 (in Chinese). Retrieved September 16, 2019, from http://www.nhc.gov.cn/guihuaxxs/s10743/201806/44e3cdfe11fa4c7f928c879d435b6a18.shtml.

National Health Commission. (2020). Functions of the National Health Commission of the PRC (in Chinese). Retrieved October 21, 2020, from http://www.nhc.gov.cn/wjw/jgzn/201809/3f4e1cf5cd104ca8a8275730ab072be5.shtm

O'Toole, P. W., & Paoli, M. (2017). The Contribution of Microbial Biotechnology to Sustainable Development Goals: Microbiome Therapies. *Microbial Biotechnology, 10*(5). https://doi.org/10.1111/1751-7915.12752.

Ping An (2020). Use Case of Smart City Solutions. Retrieved October 26, 2020, from https://city.pingan.com/ (in Chinese).

PWC. (2020). Epidemic Response to COVID-19 in Pharmaceutical and Healthcare Industries, Series Issue 2.

Rocha, P., Dias, N., Santinha, G., Rodrigues, M., Queirós, A., & Rodrigues, C. (2019). Smart Cities and Healthcare: A Systematic Review. *Technologies, 7*, 58.

Rockfellow, J. D. (1994). Wild Cards: Preparing for the Big One. *The Futurist, 28*(1), 14.

Sina Finance. (2019). China Became the World's Second Largest Pharmaceutical Market. Retrieved October 21, 2020, from https://finance.sina.com.cn/roll/2019-12-30/doc-iihnzahk0912632.shtml.

State Council. (2015). Technology Road Mapping for Strategic Important Sectors in Manufacture China 2025. Retrieved October 19, 2020, from http://www.cm2025.org/uploadfile/2016/0321/20160321015412313.pdf (in Chinese).

State Council. (2016). Promulgation of the 13th Five Year Plan for further deployment of IT in China. Retrieved October 17, 2020, from http://www.gov.cn/zhengce/content/2016-12/27/content_5153411.htm (in Chinese).

State Council. (2017). State Council Notice on the Issuance of the New Generation Artificial Intelligence Development Plan. Retrieved from http://www.gov.cn/zhengce/content/2017-07/20/content_5211996.htm [in Chinese].

State Council. (2017). State Council's Plan for the Development of New Generation Artificial Intelligence. http://www.gov.cn/zhengce/content/2017-07/20/content_5211996.htm

Sun, S., Yu, K., Xie, Z., & Pan, X. (2020). China Empowers Internet Hospital to Fight Against COVID-19. *Journal of Infection, 81*(1), 67–68.

Tan, X., Wi, Q., & Shao, H. (2018). Global Commitments and China's Endeavors to Promote Health and Achieve Sustainable Development Goals. *Journal of Health, Population and Nutrition, 37*(8), 2–4.

Whitmore, A., Agarwal, A., & Xu, L. (2014). The Internet of Things—A survey of topics and trends. *Information Systems Frontiers, 17*(2), 261–274.

Wong, D. (2020, July 31). China's Healthcare Industry: Opportunities in Telemedicine and Digital Healthcare. *China Briefing*. Retrieved from https://www.china-briefing.com/news/china-investment-outlook-telemedicine-digital-healthcare-industry/.

World Bank. (2018). Data on Healthcare Expenditures as Percentage of GDP, Healthcare Out of Pocket Payment Ratio in Healthcare Expenditures, Life Expectancy and Age Dependency Ratio. Retrieved September 16, 2019, from https://data.worldbank.org/indicator/SP.POP.DPND?locations=CN.

World Bank and DRC. (2019). *Innovative China. New Drivers of Growth*. Washington, DC: World Bank.

World Economic Forum and Boston Consulting Group. (2017). Value in Healthcare Transformation for Health System Laying the Foundation. Retrieved September 16, 2019, from http://www3.weforum.org/docs/WEF_Insight_Report_Value_Healthcare_Laying_Foundation.pdf.

Wu, D., Hesketh, T., Shu, H., Lian, W., Tang, W., & Tian, J. (2019). Description of an Online Hospital Platform, China. *Bulletin of the World Health Organization, 97*, 578–579.

Xinhua. (2019). East China Opens Life Sciences Park for Global Healthcare Innovation, Collaboration. *XinhuaNet*. Retrieved from http://www.xinhuanet.com/english/2019-09/08/c_138375934.htm.

Xinhua Newsnet. (2020). Ping An's Smart Health Solutions and Its Application in Shenzhen. Retrieved October 26, 2020, from http://www.xinhuanet.com/money/2020-09/11/c_1126482182.htm (in Chinese).

Yip, W., Fu, H., Chen, A. T., Zhai, T., Jian, W., Xu, R., et al. (2019). 10 Years of Health-Care Reform in China: Progress and Gaps in Universal Health Coverage. *Lancet, 394*, 1192–1204.

CHAPTER 7

Chinese Commercial Aircraft Manufacturing Policy: The View from the Commanding Heights

John R. McIntyre and James R. Hoadley

Abstract The chapter considers the Chinese commercial aircraft manufacturing sector as one of the commanding heights of a global leading manufacturing economy. It reviews the technological and policy pathways in manufacturing world-class commercial aircraft. Authors conclude that China seems poised to repeat in aviation what it has done in train travel—to become the world's largest market. The original projections were for that to occur by 2024. COVID-19 has altered this pace. Unlike China's achievements in its extensive high-speed rail network, China is facing the realization that its civilian skies are filled with commercial planes made in places like Toulouse, France or Everett, Washington. The national government wants Chinese-made planes serving Chinese passengers on its air routes in China.

J. R. McIntyre • J. R. Hoadley (✉)
Georgia Tech CIBER, Scheller College of Business, Atlanta, GA, USA
e-mail: john.mcintyre@scheller.gatech.edu; james.hoadley@scheller.gatech.edu

F. Spigarelli, J. R. McIntyre (eds.), *The New Chinese Dream*, Palgrave Studies of Internationalization in Emerging Markets, https://doi.org/10.1007/978-3-030-69812-6_7

Keywords Commercial aircraft • Aircraft manufacturing • Structural changes of the industry

7.1 Introduction

China seems poised to repeat in aviation what it has done in train travel—to become the world's largest market. The original projections were for that to occur by 2024. COVID-19 has altered this pace. It seems certain that once air travel settles on a new normal, China will be number one. Unlike China's achievements in its extensive high-speed rail network, China is facing the realization that its civilian skies are filled with commercial planes made in places like Toulouse, France or Everett, Washington. The national government wants Chinese-made planes serving Chinese passengers on its air routes in China. This is in line with China's industrial upgrading, economic transformation, globalization, and rise as a global geopolitical power, as analyzed in Chaps. 1 and 2. In 2006, the State Council, addressing reorganization of state-owned companies, was adamant that the "state should maintain absolute control over important industries," and commercial aircraft manufacturing was organic to the control of the commanding heights of advanced industries (State Council 2006). The ARJ21, a narrow-body regional jet, is already in service, and the C919, a competitor in size and range for the Boeing 737 and Airbus A 320 series, has multiple demonstrators in the air. The order of magnitude bears noting: COMAC (Commercial Aircraft Corporation of China) (n.d.) estimates that China will need $1.3 trillion in new planes over the next two decades, leading to 2049, the one hundredth anniversary of the People's Republic of China (Reuters 2020). In this passage, we examine the Chinese aerospace industry and how it has been influenced by Chinese industrial policy.

7.2 The Current Commercial Aviation Market in China

The growth of China's air market has been tremendous. Even with the advent of COVID-19, it is still on target in three years to become the world's largest in passenger volume (see Fig. 7.1). Chinese passenger

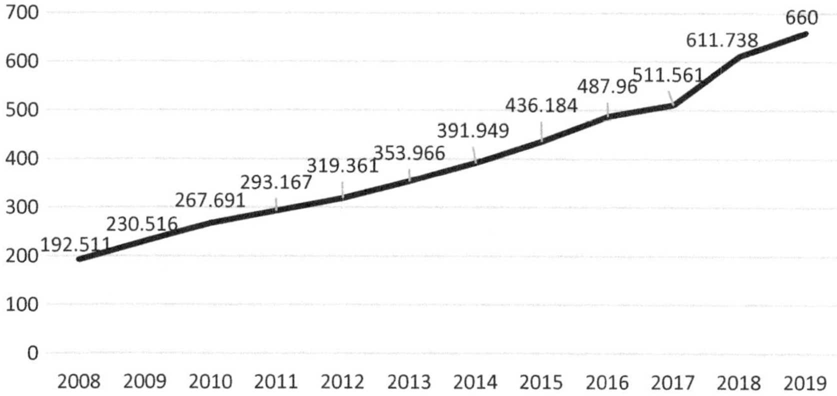

Fig. 7.1 Passenger volume in China (person mN). (Source: Civil Aviation Administration of China)

growth from 2018 to 2038 is expected to grow at over 1 1/2 percentage points higher than the global average. This is despite significant competition from one of the world's fastest growing and largest high-speed rail networks which carried over ten billion passengers in 2018.

The Chinese government is also continuing its plans to grow aviation-related infrastructure with a construction target of two hundred and fifteen new airports by 2035, effectively doubling the number of airports in China (see Fig. 7.2). All the more remarkable as these projects are moving forward in spite of momentary decreases in passenger traffic in the wake of Covid-19. According to figures released by the CAAC (Civil Aviation Administration of China), the annual growth rate of passengers in China slowed for the past three years from 13% in 2017 to 7.9% in 2019. Cargo volumes have also decreased to 75.26 billion tons which is a rise of only 1.9% from the year prior and well below the 4.6% of 2018 and 5.7% of 2017. Passenger volumes at Shanghai Pudong International Airport have been declining since 2015.

7.3 Chinese Commercial Aviation Production

Since the advent of the People's Republic of China, its government has desired to produce military aircraft domestically. Commercial aircrafts were a lower priority and their development was originally begun under

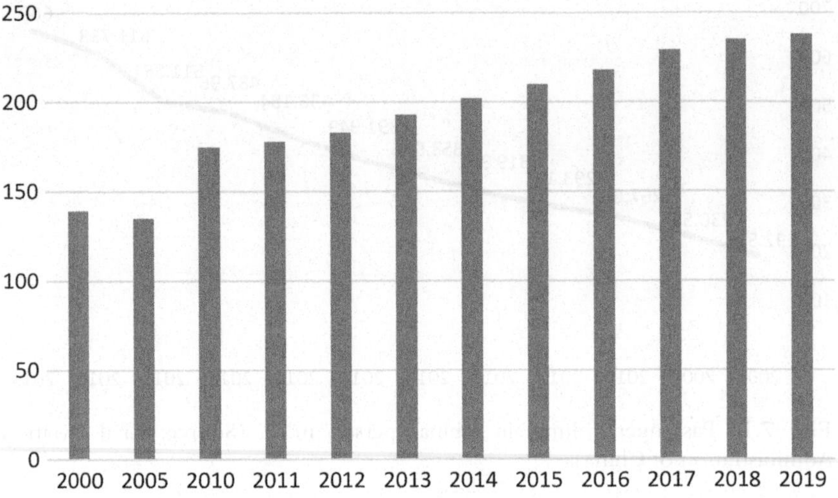

Fig. 7.2 Number of civil airports in China 2000–2019. (Source: Civil Aviation Administration of China)

the aegis of military supervision. China's first domestic jet the Y 10 was designed to be a competitor to the Boeing 707. Test flights were completed successfully in the 1980's but the plane's cost was markedly higher than its Boeing and Airbus competitors and manufacturing was halted due to design and cost issues (Barwick et al. 2020).

After the Y-10 failure in 1983, Beijing planners created a three-step long-term path to grow the commercial jet industry, aiming eventually to complete local development without foreign assistance. China then reluctantly turned to the international joint venture option to speed up the process of eventual full production autonomy. It proved a harder road to travel than anticipated. The target date to complete domestic development and production was 2010. The initial phase began in 1985 when SAIC (Shanghai Aviation Industrial Corp.) agreed with McDonnell Douglas to assemble the MD 82 narrow body airliner from kits. Between 1986 and 1994, thirty-five MD 80 series jets were assembled in China, including five exported back to the United States. There was a plan to assemble the larger MD 90 aircraft but McDonald Douglas' merger with Boeing ended that production line. In 1997, China entered a consortium with Airbus and Singapore technologies to develop A-100 seat regional jet that would be called the AE-100. This program was ended when Airbus pulled out in the wake of the Asian financial crisis (Levine 2015).

In an attempt to stimulate growth in the aviation industry, Beijing oversaw the creation of AVIC (Aviation Industry Corporation of China) as a conglomerate, with half a million employees globally and twenty seven listed companies. Quickly, AVIC was divided into halves, AVIC 1 and AVIC 2. The intention for this division was to create competition internally in China, but it was unsuccessful at this, as one settled on competing in the military aircraft space and the other focused on civilian airframes, transports, and helicopters. Therefore, in 2008, the Chinese government remerged the two companies with the intention of a reorganization (Crane et al. 2014). These hesitant strategic moves are reflective of the external challenges facing state-owned enterprises (SOEs). Yet SOEs are essential in maintaining central government control and achieving strategic objectives but also in creating powerful national champions promoting China's influence as international multinational actors (Naughton 2018).

The newly merged corporation was given the explicit task of becoming one of the world's leading aviation companies. The catch phrase used for this strategic "split and re-merge" move was "two integrations, three news, five transformations, and one trillion". The one trillion was the revenue target in renminbi for the year 2020. This was a highly ambitious target because the exchange rate for one trillion renminbi equals out 260 billion US dollars while Boeing and Airbus combined totaled only 100 billion dollars in revenue at the time (Crane et al. 2014). The two integrations referred to blending global aviation production chain into regional economic development spheres. The three "news" refer to novel emphases on value creation, business model innovation, and integrated network construction. Finally, the five transformations addressed slower-paced processes such as market-oriented reforms, specialized consolidations, capitalized operations, globalized development, and commercialized growth (Crane et al. 2014).

After the merger of AVIC 1 and AVIC 2, COMAC was spun off from AVIC in May 2008 to create a commercial aviation manufacturer mimicking Boeing and Airbus. COMAC became a somewhat more independent corporation to design, assemble, and manufacture China's indigenous commercial airliners. COMAC produces only in the commercial aviation space, both to make it more competitive and to hedge the risk of U.S. export controls and similar barriers to its integration within the global aviation market (Freifeld and Alper 2020). The issue of U.S. export controls on U.S. origin engine components sold to China is a salient one, in the wake of the Trump Administration's sweeping reform embodied in the U.S. Export Control Reform Act of 2018, now including under its purview many conventional manufacturing industries. It would appear that U.S. government agencies, in the context of the Airbus-Boeing global market competition, have reached, at present, the conclusion that this type of well-established technology exports does not pose a security risk as in other sectors of technology rivalry, such as information technology and communications, where export controls are stringent and expanding. This decision reflects an assessment of the general state of advancement of the Chinese large civilian aircraft industry. Cybersecurity controls, however, remain stringent to insure that state-of-the-art innovations are not leaked.

COMAC's initial approach was to manufacture the ARJ-21 and design and manufacture the C919. The ARJ-21 was designed as a 100-seat regional jet to take the place of aircraft like the MD 80 and some offerings from Bombardier and Embraer. The C919 was designed as a narrow body jet but slightly larger to compete in the same field as the Boeing 737 and Airbus A320 series. AVIC serves as a key domestic supplier of parts to COMAC.

The ARJ-21 is very similar in appearance and size to the MD 80 that was manufactured under contract, as well as the larger MD-90 that was planned but cancelled. Consistent with Beijing's stated desire to integrate Chinese aviation manufacturing into the global industry, many subsystems were outsourced to foreign manufacturers including GE, Safran, Rockwell, and Honeywell. The ARJ 21 had its first in-service flight in 2016 and is currently in use by approximately ten airlines and lease services, all based in China.

International joint ventures between Chinese manufacturers and Western avionics firms are not new, dating back to 1996, if not earlier, with Pratt & Whitney. In the early 2000's, Harbin Aircraft Industries group attempted a joint venture with Embraer to assemble the ERJ-145, a regional jet. The Harbin manufacturing facility was able to begin delivery in 2004 but only able to produce twenty four aircraft a year at its peak and a final delivery of only forty one aircraft before production ceased in 2011. In September 2008, a joint venture between Airbus and a Chinese consortium was created to perform final assembly of A320 jets from Airbus. The first aircraft was delivered in 2009 and the one hundredth in 2012. These international joint ventures have buttressed Chinese progress in avionics, allowing some leapfrogging in certain production lines, but

	Component	Manufacturer	Country
A	Tail & Wings	AVIC	PRC
B	Flight Data Recorder	GE	US
C	Fuel System	Parker	US
D	Fire Detection	Kidde	UK
E	Fuselage Aluminum	Arconic	US
F	Landing Gear, Wing de-icing	Liebherr	Germany
G	Wheels, Brakes, Communications, Navigation	Honeywell	US
H	Tires	Michelin	France
I	Engines	CFM	US/France
J	Thrust Reversers	Safran	France
K	Weather Radar	Rockwell	US

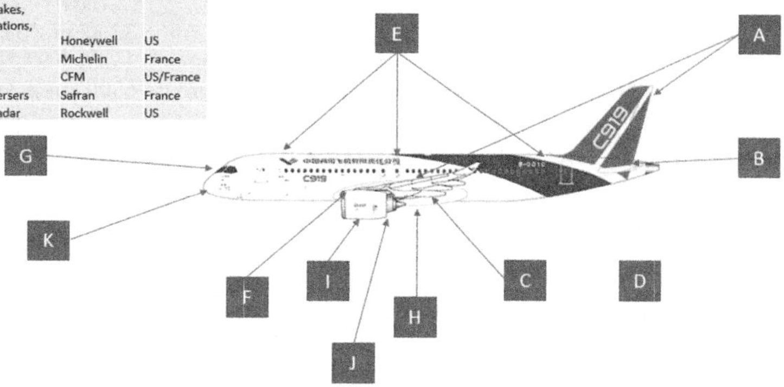

Fig. 7.3 C919 selected suppliers. (Authors from COMAC Website)

have also evidenced the typical issues encountered in joint venturing with Chinese state-owned enterprises. Hence, they can be assessed as a mixed success.

COMAC's C919, launched in 2009, is the next phase of indigenization of Chinese aviation manufacturing. The C919 is intended to serve as a substitute for the 737 and A320 jets from Boeing and Airbus respectively (see Fig. 7.3) The C919 has a number of prototypes conducting test flights, and there was a plan prior to COVID-19 to introduce the C919 into commercial service in 2020, but that has now been delayed to 2021. Production goals for the C919 are one hundred fifty aircraft per year which is one third of China's domestic annual demand. Many personnel have been shifted from the ARJ-21 to the C919 program. The current trade dispute between the United States and China was seen as an impediment as the primary engine supplier is CFM, a Franco-American consortium between GE and Safran Aircraft Engines. However, the clear separation between COMAC and military production allowed engine sales to be approved in April 2020. Table 7.1 shows the specifications of the C919 relative to its Boeing and Airbus rivals to provide technical context for COMAC's targets.

Table 7.1 Specifications of the C919 relative to its Boeing and Airbus rivals

	C919	*737–800*	*A320neo*
Passengers	168 (1-class) / 158 (2-class)	160 (1-class) 184 (max)	195 (1-class) / 165 (2-class)
Length	38.9 m / 127.6 ft	39.50 m / 129 ft. 7 in	37.57 m / 123 ft. 3 in
Weight	42.1 t / 92,815 lbs.	41.4 t / 91.300 lbs.	44.3 t / 97,700 lbs.
Range	4075 km / 2200 nm	2935 nmi (5436 km)	6500 km / 3500 nmi

Source: Authors from open sources

Both the ARJ 21 and C919 are alike in that their ultimate objective is not widespread commercial success but rather proof of concept with a view to full deployment. If China can design and manufacture complex technologies like modern aircraft, it makes the country less reliant upon American and European suppliers. It also allows aircraft manufacturing to move from a catching-up status industry to a leading industry much like high-speed rail and home appliances. Figure 7.3 illustrates the multinational nature of COMAC's suppliers for the C919 underlining COMAC's integration in this global industry.

There is an additional COMAC product designed to compete with the Boeing 787 and Airbus A330neo. Officially built by CRAIC, a consortium of COMAC from China and Russia's United Aircraft, and capable of carrying 440 passengers in a single-class configuration. There has, however, been significant friction between the Russian and Chinese design teams which has resulted in an announced delay in production. Part of the disagreement has been reported to be a Russian insistence on basing the fuselage on the Ilyushin Il-86 airliner, which was a 4-engine wide body, designed in the Soviet Union in the 1970's. Russia also insisted that rather than a technology transfer, Russia would only outsource assembly to COMAC. It was rejected by the Chinese. The possibility is now being discussed of China going it alone, with engines supplied by CFM or Rolls Royce, as China presently does not have an adequate domestic engine of the power and size required (Chen 2020).

7.4 Chinese Commercial Aviation Policy

Industrial policy has been a reform instrument in China since its opening up to the world, making possible China's development from an imperative planned economy to a "market economy with Chinese characteristics (see

Chap. 1). "Beijing has retained a "whole-of-government" approach reminiscent of "dirigisme" in growing its domestic commercial aviation industry. Because Beijing exerts centralized authority over the operation of state-owned enterprises (SOEs), this organic approach is rooted in broad policy priority declarations emanating from the Chinese State Council and refined further by successive directives and documents by various ministries and local government entities. There are six promulgated government plans deserving attention which define Chinese commercial aircraft manufacturing policy. They are fleshed out below (Ohlandt et al. 2017):

- *National 5-year plans.* Development priorities set by the State Council call for breakthroughs in civilian aviation engine technology so far dependent on foreign sources;
- *Identified Strategic Emerging Industries.* Two documents stand out, the "Decision on Accelerating the Cultivation and Development of Strategic Emerging Industries" and "Development Plan for Strategic Emerging Industries of the 14th Five-Year Plan." They list goals and aspirations for Strategic Emerging Industries considered the most salient for Chinese civilian aviation;
- *National Medium to Long Term Plan for Civil Aviation.* It calls for the domestically manufactured civilian aircraft to account for no less than 5 percent of China's total civilian aviation market by 2020. It also stresses the domestic development of a domestic turbine-engine sector narrow-body aircraft;
- *The 5-year plan for Chinese Civil Aviation Development* (currently in its 14th iteration). Calls for China to enhance the safety, popularity, and globalization of China's civilian aviation industry, a critical issue to certify Chinese made civilian aircraft both for the domestic and international markets which would hold back commercialization of the aircraft;
- *Made in China 2025.* Released in 2015, it calls on China to speed up research and development in large aircraft, including widebody passenger aircraft, and to enhance international cooperation. It sets a target, perhaps unrealistically, that general-purpose aircraft components should capture between 30 and 40 percent of the domestic market share by 2025. These are steep goals for the Chinese aviation industry to climb and industry experts have expressed doubts (South China Morning Post 2018; Dufour 2019).

Figure 7.4 illustrates the complex organizational structure and decision-making process for COMAC as it addresses global strategic corporate choices. Comparatively speaking, the Boeing and Airbus Group duopoly, dependent as each may be on some government support, is relatively more agile. China has been debating the latitude it will grant its national champions as they become international corporate actors. Implicit in the 2025 initiative and its longer term 2049 centennial version is that government should follow the practices of firms in developed countries, encouraging innovation, while supporting such industries through government purchases. A clear resolution of this organizational dilemma does not seem to avail in the foreseeable future.

It is China's stated long-term goal to become a fully developed country that is prosperous, powerful, democratic and culturally advanced by 2049, the year when the People's Republic of China celebrates its centenary (see Chap. 1). These lofty ideals can be pragmatically translated into achieving global leadership in technology and heavy manufacturing, reprising the challenges of Made in China 2025. Selling complex capital goods on the global market is desirable but substituting domestic manufacturers for imported goods is an even greater end goal, given the current trade war between the United States and China.

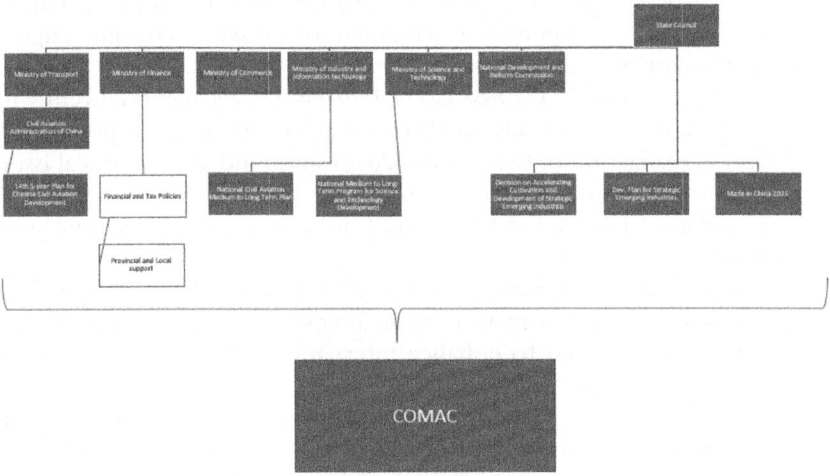

Fig. 7.4 Organizational structure and decision-making process for COMAC. (Source: Authors from open sources)

This conflictual situation casts doubts upon the availability and cost of American made aircraft and components. It leaves open a door for the Europeans to expand their market penetration, possibly at the expense of a rift with the United States if this brewing Sino-US conflict takes on the appearance of what some term a "cold war." It also raises the specter of autarky and import substitution in what is a supremely global industry. Plainly, by producing its own and demonstrating its autonomous capability, China can both move down the experience curve, avoid paying tariffs, and sending money out of the country. In this regard, the Chinese approach to commercial aviation may be seen as comparable to high speed rail.

Only a couple of decades ago China had practically no presence in high speed rail. Today, China is one of the most competitive manufacturers in the world (Mok 2019). China's aviation offerings are comparable to its high-speed rail offerings: they do not implement new technology, they are not particularly more efficient, and they are not remarkably safe or budget conscious. The difficulty and complexity in developing an industry ecosystem and supply chains necessary to respond to the manufacturing base's needs is a long and drawn out process. By investing in vehicles like the ARJ 21 and the C 919, China is attempting to shorten the development curve. China's carefully crafted international joint ventures allow it to develop some competency in the aviation industry but they do not allow China to develop complex engineering skills. China is seeking to develop a domestic base of aeronautical engineers able to design greater and better aircraft.

Made in China 2025 is the highest profile initiative, reconfirmed by the 2049 longer-term societal and economic objectives. Released in 2015, it is composed of three ten-year phases, the first of which is to become a major world manufacturing power by 2025. The second phase is to become an intermediate-level competitor by 2035 and, finally, to become the world's leading manufacturer by 2049, alarming its Western rivals. It sets out ten key industry sectors which include "next generation" IT, robotics and aviation and aerospace, among others, as well as operating principles. It is noteworthy that the aviation and aerospace directive is not narrowly limited to aircraft; it includes plans to triple the number of Chinese satellites in orbit, for example (Wu and Tse 2018).

The challenge in producing the Chinese Way is that the players as government-owned industries are operating on the basis of compartmentalization of information. In order to develop a robust aerospace industry, vital information for engineering and production must be shared more openly among suppliers. State-owned enterprises in China do not do transparency well (Ohlandt et al. 2017). Still, China may be able to compete on the basis of price as its cost structure theoretically is lower. It might thus allow COMAC-produced commercial aircraft to sell in parts of the world where low cost is the highest priority. Thus, COMAC might become the jet supplier to frontier economies and developing countries, if it can satisfy world-class certifying safety standards. The Boeing 737 Max crisis has created a potential opening for COMAC that had not so far existed. It remains to be seen, however, if falling global passenger volumes in the wake of COVID-19 have closed that door. It is worth noting that the ARJ 21 and C919 are only certified for commercial use in China. No certification for these aircraft in Europe or North America has been granted. American and European aviation authorities may use their influence to try to keep Chinese aircraft from flying outside of China.

Finally, the biggest obstacle for COMAC to overcome is the development of a support structure for COMAC manufactured aircraft. Boeing and Airbus planes have a large and robust network of qualified pilots, qualified service personnel, and mechanics as well as a well-honed network of parts suppliers. COMAC at present has almost none of these features outside of China. The most concrete quantitative goal of Made in China 2025 remains to reduce China's reliance on foreign technological components to increase domestic and international demand share.

In the twenty first century, industrial policy has become innovation policy. Neither the ARJ21 and C919 are particularly innovative as vehicles of the future. In the realm of high-speed rail, China became competitive because a rail system is a closed loop. If one purchases high speed rail from China, the Chinese suppliers will install the entire system from rails to stations to switching mechanisms to the train sets themselves. Aircraft, on the other hand, are much more mobile and substitutions can be made much more easily. It can be said that the aviation industry has much more in common with the automotive industry. For many of the same reasons that China is yet to be a global force to reckoned with in the automobile sector, it faces many similar barriers to entry for aviation. Competitors can enter freely and easily. The devices to use the network can easily be swapped in and out. Another point of comparison is worthy of note: China is extremely competitive in the global shipbuilding industry because of massive subsidies. Barwick, Zahur, and Kalouptsidi found that the Chinese shipping industry subsisted on subsidies as net profits increased only one-fifth the value of the subsidies themselves. China's electric production industry similarly is highly inefficient. The standard for power networks backup is 15% beyond peak load. In many provinces in China, the excess capacity available for backup is 90% of peak load.

According to the World Bank and OECD, China's total factor productivity growth in China has been one third of what it was prior to the 2008 financial crisis (Brandt et al. 2020). It seems that China's industrial policy is focused on market share rather than developing competitiveness. This very much echoes the hazard of the infant industry argument in trade policy: when is an industry no longer an infant industry? In more democratic nations, there is often pressure from voters to reduce expenditures. The theoretical rationale for deploying industrial policies is to correct market failures which are rampant, especially in developing countries. In China's case and in its commercial aircraft industry, one finds evidence of significant government distortions, no doubt the legacy of central planning, that must gradually be resolved through more market-oriented reforms. How to distinguish good from bad industrial policy particularly in a country undergoing an economic transition is not an easy question to answer.

A further question relates to the issue of Chinese innovation. In the past, Chinese innovation consisted primarily of duplication or leap frogging the innovatory process through intellectual property theft, as termed in the West. China has recently enacted measures to make the country more compliant with international expectations of intellectual property protection for items that are not deemed strategic. China, however, has selected the aerospace industry as an industry sector in which it wants to be globally competitive. Thus, the dilemma is one of improving China's record on innovation. Should China focus more on basic research or should China overhaul its innovation system itself to reduce misallocation of innovatory resources and better protect intellectual property rights as it catches up? In certain sectors, China has achieved global innovatory leadership: high-speed rail, mobile payments, e-commerce and bike-sharing technology, China's Four Great New Inventions (An 2017). Commercial aircraft manufacturing remains an open question.

Chinese "innovation" was initially characterized by the shanzhai method. At first and due in part to the relative poverty of rural China, a system of cheap "knock off" products was developed. This brought forth an organic system which works more like open source, where copies are freely mixed and adapted to create products which are not wholly new, but not an attempted copy of the original source(s) either (Wang 2018). The earlier ARJ 21 is very close to the MD-80 that was manufactured under contract. In other words, an old-style shanzhai near copy. The C919 is not a copy of either the A320 or 737. It more closely exemplifies the new-style of shanzhai. The C919 is not a design from scratch with Western design inputs. Crowdstrike has reported that COMAC has been connected with industrial espionage related to engine producer CFM international, as well as other suppliers in the C919 supply chain (NDIA, Editorial Board 2020). What remains to be seen is whether COMAC can produce a successful aircraft in the C919, and then produce a pipeline of new innovations in the successor aircrafts. Then, and only then, will COMAC be an internationally competitive commercial aircraft manufacturer, and the final phase of China's international industrial policy be realized: to turn industrial gaps into opportunities and not vulnerabilities.

References

An, E. (2017, August 8). Spotlight: China's 'Four Great New Inventions' in Modern Times. *Xinhuanet.*

Barwick, P. J., Kalouptsidi, M., & Zahur, N. B. (2020). *China's Industrial Policy, An Empirical Evaluation.* Cornell: NBER.

Brandt, L., Litwack, J., Mileva, E., Wang, L., Zhang, Y., & Zhao, L. (2020, June). *China's Productivity Slowdown and Future Growth Potential.* Policy Research Working Paper 9298. World Bank. Retrieved from http://documents1.worldbank.org/curated/en/839401593007627879/pdf/Chinas-Productivity-Slowdown-and-Future-Growth-Potential.pdf.

Chen, F. (2020, September 28). China-Russia Big Jet Project Faces Turbulence. *Asia Times.* Retrieved from https://asiatimes.com/2020/09/china-russia-big-jet-project-faces-turbulence/.

COMAC. (n.d.). Tier 1 Supplier, Commercial Aircraft Corporation of China, Inc. Tier 1 Supplier Commercial Aircraft Corporation of China, Ltd. Commercial Aircraft of China, Ltd. Retrieved October 13, 2020, from http://english.comac.cc/suppliers/t1/index.shtml.

Crane, K., Luoto, J. E., Harold, S. W., Yang, D., Berkowitz, S. K., & Wang, X. (2014). Net Assessment of the Effectiveness of China's Industrial Policies for Commercial Aviation Manufacturing. In *The Effectiveness of China's Industrial Policies in Commercial Aviation Manufacturing* (pp. 55–70). Santa Monica, CA: RAND Corporation. Retrieved September 24, 2020, from http://www.jstor.org/stable/10.7249/j.ctt6wq85j.13.

Dufour, J- F. (2019). *COMAC C919: A Realistic Assessment of Commercial Perspectives.* DCA Chine Analyse, Special Report: 09/2019.

Freifeld, K., & Alper, A. (2020, February 15). U.S. Weighs Blocking GE Engine Sales for China's New Airplanes: Sources. *Reuters*. Retrieved from https://www.reuters.com/article/us-usa-china-aircraft/u-s-weighs-blocking-ge-engine-sales-for-chinas-new-airplane-sources-idUSKBN2090SG.

Lee, A. (2018, October 29). China's Aviation Industry Has a Steep Climb to 'Made in China 2025' Goals. *South China Morning Post*. Retrieved from https://www.scmp.com/business/article/2170746/chinas-aviation-industry-has-steep-climb-made-china-2025-goals.

Levine, D. A. (2015). The Dragon Takes Flight: China's Aviation Policy, Achievements, and International Implications. *China Studies Series, 31*.

Mok, W. (2019, December 11). China's High-Speed Rail Makes It a Fierce Economic Competitor. *South China Morning Post*. Retrieved from https://www.scmp.com/comment/opinion/article/3041150/how-high-speed-rail-has-made-china-fierce-competitor-global-economy.

Naughton, B. (2018). State Enterprise Reform Today. In R. Garnaut, L. Song, & C. Fang (Eds.), *China's 40 Years of Reform and Development, 1978–2018*. Canberra, Australia: ANU Press.

NDIA, Editorial Board. (n.d.). *How China Conducts Cyber Industrial Espionage*. NDIA. Retrieved September 24, 2020, from https://www.ndia.org/policy/recent-posts/2019/11/4/how-china-conducts-cyber-industrial-espionage.

Ohlandt, C., Morris, L., Thompson, J., Chan, A., & Scobell, A. (2017). *Rep. Chinese Investment in U.S. Aviation*. RAND Corporation. Retrieved from https://www.rand.org/pubs/research_reports/RR1755.html.

Reuters. (2020, September 16). Boeing Raises 20-Year Forecast for China Aircraft Demand. *Reuters*. Retrieved from https://www.reuters.com/article/us-china-aviation-boeing/boeing-raises-20-year-forecast-for-china-aircraft-demand-idUSKBN1W207X.

State Council. (2006). *Notice on Pushing Forward the Adjustment of State Stocks and Reorganization of SOEs*. State Council General Office 206-No. 97. Retrieved from http://www.gov.cn/gongbao/content/2007/content_503385.htm.

Wang, X. R. (2018, August 24). New Shanzhai 山寨 (Shanzhai). *Wired*. Condé Nast. Retrieved from https://www.wired.com/beyond-the-beyond/2018/08/new-shanzhai-%E5%B1%B1%E5%AF%A8-shanzhai/.

Wu, J., & Tse, A. (2018, September 11). Why 'Made in China 2025' Triggered the Wrath of President Trump. *South China Morning Post*. Retrieved from https://multimedia.scmp.com/news/china/article/made-in-China-2025/index.html.

CHAPTER 8

The Semiconductor Industry: A Strategic Look at China's Supply Chain

Yin Li

Abstract Restricting China's access to advanced semiconductor technology has become the U.S. government's chokepoint strategy in the emerging hi-tech cold war. The development of an indigenous semiconductor supply chain is increasingly vital for China's next stage of development. This chapter documents China's experience of semiconductor industry policy and development, and evaluates key Chinese players in the IC supply chain and their technological capabilities. A strategic look at the supply chain shows that China's semiconductor industry is resilient even under the U.S. pressure, though significant weakness remains.

Keywords US-China Technology War • Semiconductor industry • China supply chain • Indigenous innovation

Y. Li (✉)
School of International Relations and Public Affairs, Fudan University, Shanghai, China
e-mail: yinli@fudan.edu.cn

F. Spigarelli, J. R. McIntyre (eds.), *The New Chinese Dream*, Palgrave Studies of Internationalization in Emerging Markets,
https://doi.org/10.1007/978-3-030-69812-6_8

8.1 Introduction

In the middle of a global pandemic in 2020, access to advanced semiconductor technology has emerged as a hot battlefield in the US-China technology rivalry (Feng and Li 2020). On May 15, 2020, the U.S. Department of Commerce banned Huawei Technologies, the Chinese telecommunication technology giant, from acquiring semiconductors designed and produced with American technologies, after one year of putting Huawei on the BIS Entity List of export control. Four months later, the Commerce Department set more export controls on China's top chipmaker, Semiconductor Manufacturing International Corporation (SMIC), requiring U.S. companies to obtain licenses before selling specific technologies and equipment to SMIC. Although the U.S. government had previously issued export bans to Chinese semiconductor companies (e.g. the addition of Fujian Jinhua to Entity List over alleged technology theft in October 2018), targeting China's leading technology companies is clearly a dramatic escalation of existing tensions. From both within and outside of China, there is a growing consent that restricting China's access to advanced semiconductor technology has become the U.S. government's chokepoint strategy to inhibit Chinese technological development and maintain American industrial leadership.

Semiconductors are the backbone of advanced information technology. These tiny electronic devices enable everything in a modern society, from computers and cellphones, to home appliances and automobiles, to robotics and power grids. While China has become the world's largest electronics producer, the country relies heavily on foreign companies to supply this critical technology. Since 2006, the import of semiconductors including integrated circuits (IC) and other types of silicon devices have exceeded crude oil to become China's largest imported commodity. China's annual import value for ICs had reached 200 billion U.S. dollars by 2013 and 300 billion dollars by 2018.

China has long pursued independence in semiconductor technology (Hu 2006; Lazonick and Li 2013; Li 2016). As tensions with the U.S. increase, it is only logical to assume China would double down on a path of indigenous development. In 2016, China's President Xi Jinping said, "having core technology controlled by others is the greatest hidden danger" (Xi 2016). In 2020, President Xi again called for efforts to pursue "technology that is strategic and takes long-term commitment" in industries "relying on imported components, parts, and raw materials" (Xi 2020).

In this chapter, an assessment of the current status of the Chinese semiconductor industry in 2020 is provided, along with its ability to counter increasingly aggressive U.S. policy for technology competition. To understand the strength and weakness of the Chinese semiconductor industry, one needs to examine its historical trajectory of development. In the following parts of the chapter, I document China's semiconductor industry policy and development from the beginning of the People's Republic to present days. I then evaluate key Chinese players in the IC supply chain and their technology capabilities. Based on the analyses, policy implications are offered.

8.2 Chinese Semiconductor Industry Policy and Development

China was among the first handful of nations that committed to research and develop semiconductor technology in the twentieth century. In 1956, the Chinese government's "March Towards Science" campaign identified semiconductor as a key priority for China's future. Throughout the 1950s, scientists returning from the West had established semiconductor physics departments in elite Chinese universities, including Peking University, Fudan University, Jilin University, Xiamen University, and Nanjing University. In 1965, Chinese researchers developed their first piece of integrated circuit (IC), only seven years after the IC was invented by Texas Instrument in 1958 (Li 2017).

Since the economic reform and opening-up in 1978, China adopted a strategy to rapidly establish a modern semiconductor industry using imported technology. In the early 1980s, Chinese national and local governments spent some 1.3 billion renminbi (or 150 million US dollar) to import thirty three sets of second-hand semiconductor production equipment to upgrade twenty four key enterprises. In 1982, the State Council established the Lead Group for Electronics, Computers, and Large-Scale IC, a first high-level government body for inter-ministry coordination and strategic industry policy making for promoting the semiconductor industry. In 1984, the Lead Group was renamed to State Council Lead Group for the Promotion of Electronics Industry. One of the key decisions the Lead Group made was to consolidate the state's efforts in a small number of leading firms for industry development and upgrade. Between 1988 and 1995, China established five relatively large-scale, key state-owned semiconductor enterprises, including Huajing Electronics (Wuxi, Jiangsu), Huayue Microelectronics (Shaoxing, Zhejiang), Shanghai Belling, Shanghai Philips, and Beijing Shougang-NEC (Simon and Rehn 1987; Li 2017).

In 1990, China launched its first state project for IC industry promotion, Project 908, targeting the LSI (Large Scale Integration) technology of building transistors at sub-micron nodes. The Chinese government allocated 2 billion renminbi to Huajing to build an IC production line capable of processing 12,000 6-inch wafers per month using 0.8–1.2 um process technology transferred from AT&T-Lucent during the period of the eighth five-year plan (1991–1995). Unfortunately, the slow decision-making process within the government caused a lengthy delay to the project. By the time the 6-inch fab went online in 1997, its technology was already trailing behind. After years of joint venture with Hong Kong-based CSMC, Huajing was eventually acquired by China Resource Group in 2003 (Fuller 2016; Mays 2013).

In 1995, the newly established Ministry of Electronics Industry launched another major state project, Project 909, in upgrading domestic semiconductor industry. The centerpiece of Project 909 involves an investment of over 10 billion renminbi (or 1.2 billion US dollar) to build an 8-inch production line using VLSI technology at 0.35–0.5 um process nodes and having a monthly output of 20,000 wafers. The project was carried out through an international joint venture between Shanghai Huahong Group and Japan's NEC. The Huahong Group has since become a major IC foundry, even though Huahong was often criticized for relying on Japanese management and engineers to achieve early success (Hu 2006; Fuller 2016).

In anticipating China's accession to the World Trade Organization (WTO), the State Council issued a major semiconductor industry policy document named "*Several Polices to Encourage Software and Integrated Circuits Industry Development*", also known as Document 18, in July 2000. Document 18 marked a major shift in policy tools for industry promotion, as the new policy emphasized broad-based tax incentives to encourage entries of private and foreign capital (Li 2016).

In the decade following China's WTO entry, there were major entries into the three main industrial segments of the semiconductor value chain: semiconductor design, fabrication, and packaging and testing. Thanks to China's large pool of skilled and low-cost labor, the country has become a leading player in the labor-intensive packaging and testing industries. In the IC design sectors, the number of entries increased from less than 100 in 2000 to nearly 500 by 2004. Although the majority of Chinese IC design houses are small companies competing in relatively low-end segments of the market, a selected few firms have grown into scale and closed gaps with international leaders. Driven by explosive growth of the smartphone market in the 2010s, a number of mobile chipmakers have emerged as China's leading semiconductor design houses, including Huawei's HiSilicon, Unigroup's Unisoc (merged from Spreadtrum and RDA), and Sanechips (ZTE Microelectronics).

In IC fabrication, Semiconductor Manufacturing International Corporation (SMIC) has emerged as a new national champion. Established in Pudong, Shanghai in 2000, SMIC was founded by Richard Ru-Gin Chang and a group of over 100 expatriate managers and engineers. Chang had accumulated deep experience in building foundries by previously working for Texas Instrument and running his own startups. Chang's team raised 1.48 billion US dollar of initial capital from Chinese government and international investors, including venture capital firms Walden International, Vertex Venture Holdings, H&Q Asia Pacific and Goldman Sachs. By 2004, SMIC has already become China's largest and most technologically sophisticated semiconductor foundry (Li 2016).

In 2006, the Chinese government had officially adopted "indigenous innovation" as a national strategy through the issuance of the "*Outline of the National Medium- and Long-term Programme on Science and Technology Development* (2006–2020)" (MLP) (Lazonick and Li 2013). To meet the goal of building China as an innovative nation by 2020, the Ministry of Science and Technology established a total of 16 National S&T Major Projects (also known as "Mega Projects") in key technology areas, including broadband mobile networks, advanced machinery, nuclear power, commercial aircrafts, and new drug development. Introduced in 2012, "Ultra-Large-Scale Integrated Circuit Manufacturing Equipment and Technology" is one of the sixteen Mega Projects designated to advance the development of advanced chip technology and equipment with 45 nanometer or smaller process nodes. The project has funded a broad range of R&D projects conducted by universities, research institutes, and domestic firms.

In June 2014, the State Council issued "*Guidelines to Promote National Integrated Circuit Industry*". A key strategy identified in this guideline is to focus policy support on a small number of leading domestic firms.

Three months later, the National IC Industry Investment Fund (also known as the Big Fund) was established with capital raised from 16 state entities and business firms, including the Ministry of Finance, China Development Bank Capital, and a number of state-owned investment fund and state-owned enterprises such as China Tabaco, China Mobile, and China Electronics Technology Group. By the end of 2018, the Big Fund had completed its first phase of investment, allocating a total fund of 104.7 billion renminbi to investment in all parts of the semiconductor value chain: IC design (19.7%), IC fabrication (47.8%), packaging and testing (11%), semiconductor materials (1.4%), semiconductor equipment (1.2%), and industry ecosystem (19%). The largest recipients of capital from the Big Fund investment include Tsinghua Unigroup (10 billion RMB) in IC design and manufacturing, Yangtze Memory Technologies Co (YMTC) (19 billion RMB) in memory chip manufacturing, SMIC (21 billion RMB) in IC foundry, and Jingsu Changjiang Electronics Technology (JCET) (4.6 billion RMB) in IC packaging and testing. At the same time, the first phase of the Big Fund has leveraged additional 541.5 billion RMB financing in the forms of equity investment, corporate bonds, and bank loans, including various Local IC Funds established by regional governments. By the end of 2019, the National IC Fund is launching the second phase of investment, expecting to raise over 200 billion RMB in capital. The second phase investment is expected to further strengthen weak links in China's IC supply chain, especially in semiconductor equipment and materials.

In 2015, the Chinese government released "*Made in China 2025*", as analyzed in Chaps. 1, 2 and 9, a plan to develop ten advanced manufacturing sectors by 2025, including next generation information technology, controlling instruments and robotics, aerospace and aviation equipment, maritime equipment and shipbuilding, railway equipment, energy-efficient and new-energy vehicles, electrical equipment, new materials, medical devices, and agricultural machinery. The semiconductors, especially ICs, were identified as the foundation of the next-gen IT industry. In October 2015, the State Council issued a Technical Roadmap for implementing the plan, establishing goals for the semiconductor sector to "develop the IC design industry, grow the IC manufacturing industry, upgrade the advanced packaging and testing industry, facilitate breakthroughs in the key IC equipment and materials" (State Council 2015).

In July 2020, the State Council issued "*Several Policies for Promoting the High-Quality Development of the Integrated Circuit Industry and the*

Software Industry in the New Era", a policy document that reiterates Chinese government's commitment in the industry as the U.S. pressure intensifies. This new policy document extends one of the largest tax breaks for semiconductor manufacturers with advanced sub-28 nanometer node technologies on one hand, it gives government support to facilitate equity financing for semiconductor enterprises on the other hand. In the same month, China's semiconductor national champion, SMIC, delisted from NASDAQ in 2019, launched an initial public offering (IPO) on the Shanghai Stock Exchange's STAR Market. SMIC raised 53 billion RMB in the nation's biggest IPO over the decade, providing SMIC with ample cash to invest in new fabs and R&D.

8.3 Evaluation of China's Semiconductor Supply Chain

Although China has yet to cultivate any world leading semiconductor companies, it has established presence in almost every step of chipmaking, thanks to decades of investment and development. To be fair, there are plenty of weak links in China's domestic semiconductor supply chain, especially in supporting industries such as IC manufacturing equipment, materials, and Electronic Design Automation (EDA) tools. Even the most advanced Chinese semiconductor companies are much smaller in size and technologically lagging compared to international leaders. As the U.S. is increasingly willing to cut off China's access to advanced technology, it will become challenging for China to develop a strong semiconductor industry. Nevertheless, the presence of a complete domestic semiconductor supply chain increases the chances for Chinese companies to survive under aggressive U.S. policy, and in turn, supplying the vast domestic market could be the best opportunity for Chinese semiconductor companies and equipment suppliers. Before analyzing the capabilities of leading Chinese firms in the semiconductor supply chain, the model of production in the global semiconductor industry is briefly described.

The modern semiconductor industry consists three main parts, corresponding to the three main steps in making IC chips: IC design, IC fabrication, and IC packaging & testing (Fig. 8.1), as already mentioned in the previous paragraph. Each part of the semiconductor industry is supported by a number of equipment, materials, and software industry. For instance, IC design needs specialized software of EDA tools and IP (intellectual

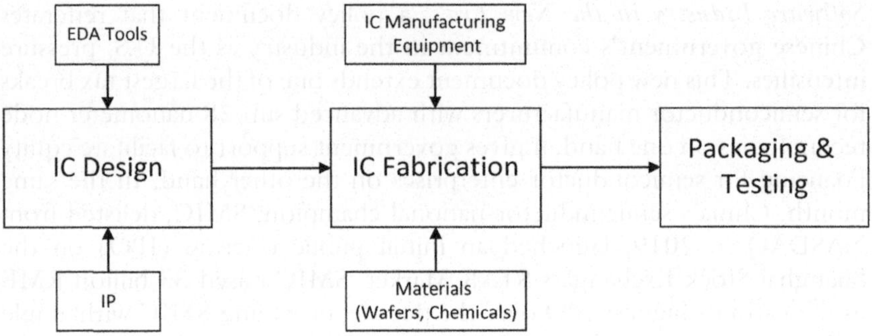

Fig. 8.1 Integrated circuits industry supply chain. (Source: Author's compilation)

property) cores supplied by specialty software companies, while IC fabrication relies on specialty equipment makers to supply advanced machinery (e.g. lithography machine) and material suppliers to provide high quality silicon wafers and various specialty chemicals.

Since the 1990s, the global semiconductor industry has become highly fragmented, in which each of the three steps in chipmaking are undertaken by different, specialized firms often located in distant parts of the world. In general, American companies such as Qualcomm, Nvidia, and AMD lead the IC design sector, while East Asia companies (i.e. TSMC and Samsung) dominates IC foundry services. Although the IDM (Integrated Device Manufacture) model of vertical integration used to be the norm, today there are few semiconductor companies that can perform all the tasks from IC design to fabrication. The exceptions include Intel, which design and manufacture high performance computer processors, and memory chip (i.e. NAND flash memory and DRAM) manufacturers that requires close integration between design and fabrication.

8.3.1 *Packaging and Testing*

China has a strong presence in the IC packaging and testing industry, accounting for over half of global production in recent years. China's strength in packaging and testing is partly driven by the labor-intensive nature of this industry, and partly facilitated by co-location with the world's largest electronics supply chain. The three largest Chinese packaging and testing firms are Jingsu Changjiang Electronics Technology

(JCET), Tianshui Huatian Microelectronics (TSHT), and Tongfu Microelectronics (TFME, formerly Nantong Fujitsu Microelectronics). These three firms can all trace their roots to state-owned electronics factories located in China's pre-reform industrial bases that were later reformed and privatized. Thanks to investment from the National IC Fund, the leading Chinese packaging and testing companies have expanded rapidly in recent years, acquired foreign competitors and their Chinese operations, and experienced significant technology upgrade. JCET, China's largest and most advanced packaging and testing firm, has been an Apple supplier since 2018.

8.3.2 IC Foundry

IC fabrication is the most capital- and technology-intensive segment of the semiconductor industry. It costs some 10 to 15 billion US dollars to construct a state-of-the-art IC fab capable of processing 12-inch wafers and fabricating chips at 7-nanometer node. With fewer and fewer companies willing to lay out the enormous capital expenditure, the global foundry capacity is increasingly concentrated in a handful of contract manufacturers, or IC foundries, that provides fabrication services to other companies.

SMIC is China's largest and most sophisticated IC foundry, the fifth largest in the world after TSMC, Samsung, Global Foundries, and UMC. Started as an internationally oriented company with investment from Silicon Valley, SMIC was able to acquire advanced machinery from the U.S. that other Chinese companies were unable to. In the mid-2000s, SMIC was able to close the technology gap with international leaders to only one generation (or less than two years). Yet, a series of lawsuits brought by TSMC over intellectual property rights violation and the difficulties in transitioning to FinFET technology for sub-14/16 nanometer process nodes have severely delayed technology development at SMIC. By the mid-2010s, SMIC was lagging the international technology frontiers for some three generations of process nodes (or 5–7 years) (Li 2016). Capital investment from the National IC Fund eventually allowed SMIC to resume its technology catch-up. SMIC is currently scaling up its 14-nanometer chip production and doing R&D for 7-naonometer process node.

Because of the exponential increases in costs and technological difficulties, there are only three companies in the world, including TSMC,

Samsung, and Intel, that have developed or are currently developing 7-nanometer or smaller process node. Even the U.S. technology leader, Intel is struggling to mass produce 7-nanometer for its computer processors. In other words, the R&D of 7 nanometer technology would be extremely challenging for SMIC. Moreover, there are additional risks from SMIC's reliance on American-made machinery. At the time of writing, SMIC is applying license from the U.S. Department of Commerce to provide foundry services to Huawei, a major domestic customer of advanced node but is blocked by the U.S. government. In addition, SMIC has significant difficulties in importing an EUV lithography machine from the Netherlands' ASML, which is a critical piece of machinery for mass producing 7-nanometer chips. Because of American-made components in the EUV machines, ASML also needs export license from the U.S. government.

8.3.3 IC Design

While foundry has become increasingly expensive, the separation of IC design and foundry has released semiconductor design companies from investing in costly machinery and facility. The introduction of fabless business model to China in the early 2000's led to waves of semiconductor startups that focus on designing chips while leveraging fabrication capabilities from domestic and international foundries. Driven by exploding demands from the electronics manufacturing industry, a number of Chinese fabless design houses have become capable and internationally competitive in their niche markets. For example, OmniVision Technologies, part of the Shanghai-based Will Semiconductor Group, is the world's third largest CMOS image sensor supplier after Sony and Samsung, supplying to leading smartphone makers including Apple, Huawei, and Xiaomi. Shenzhen-based Goodix Technology, founded in 2002, is one of the world's largest suppliers of fingerprint identification chips.

The largest Chinese fabless semiconductor companies, however, still have difficulties in competing with international leaders such as Qualcomm, Broadcom, Nvidia, and MediaTek. Telecom technology giant Huawei's inhouse semiconductor design house, HiSilicon, is currently the largest and most sophisticated Chinese semiconductor company, the only company from China Mainland that ranked among the world's top ten semiconductor companies in recent years. Yet HiSilicon does not engage in direction competition with international semiconductor firms, since it is primarily a captive supplier to Huawei's own smartphone, telecom equipment, and other electronics businesses. HiSilicon's technology capability is clearly demonstrated in delivering Kirin 9000, the world's second 5-nanometer smartphone chipset (fabricated by TSMC), only after Apple's A14. However, HiSilicon is dependent on the access to international supply chains to maintain its technology lead: it needs TSMC to fabricate advanced chips, American EDA vendors (Cadence and Synopsys) for tools of chip design, and UK-based ARM for IP cores. With the U.S. export ban on Huawei, it has become extremely challenging for HiSilicon to even maintain its current business, not to mention advancing a technology lead.

Tsinghua Unigroup's Unisoc is currently the second largest semiconductor company in China. The company was formerly Spreadtrum Communications, founded in 2001 in Shanghai as a smartphone chipset maker. In 2018, Spreadtrum was merged with RDA Microelectronics (which Unigroup acquired in 2014) to become Unisoc. Spreadtrum and RDA were two of China's most successful fabless startups that followed MediaTek's business model of supplying turn-key solutions (i.e. chipset, software, and know-how) to mobile phone manufacturers. Thanks to China's booming mobile phone industry, both Spreadtrum and RDA gained significant market shares by supplying mid- to low-end markets. With the merger of the two and further capital injection from Unigroup, Unisoc is positioned to become a national champion in IC design. However, given the fact that Unisoc has not yet broken into supply chains of any leading smartphone manufacturers, further technological upgrade at Unisoc is also challenging.

8.3.4 Memory Chip Manufacturing

Memory chips, including NAND flash memory and DRAM (dynamic random access memory) chips, are the commodity semiconductor devices widely used in modern electronics. Because of its large volume, memory chips are naturally a target of import substitution. China has made several attempts to ramp up domestic production of memory chips, but it has only achieved limited successes over the years. Both Huahong-NEC and SMIC had engaged in DRAM manufacturing in their early phase, and both exited the market due to heavy losses from high market volatility (Li 2016). More recently, Fujian Jinhua, backed by Fujian provincial government, intended to enter the DRAM market through a joint venture with UMC. The project came to a halt after Jinhua was placed in the Entity List in 2018.

China's recent success in indigenous production of memory chips is achieved by two startup companies: Yangtze Memory Technology Co. (YMTC) and ChangXin Memory Technologies (CXMT). YMTC was previously Wuhan Xinxin Semiconductor Manufacturing Co. (XMC), an IC foundry established in 2006, managed by SMIC, and a contract manufacturer of NAND flash memory for an American company Spansion (Li 2016). XMC began the R&D of 3D NAND flash memory back in 2014, but not until 2016, XMC had sufficient capital to invest in manufacturing facilities. In 2016, XMC was acquired by Tsinghua Unigroup to establish YMTC. With massive investment from Unigroup and National IC Fund, YMTC speeded up R&D and ramped up production. By 2018, YMTC began to mass produce 32-layer 3D NAND memory. In 2020, YMTC launched its indigenously developed 128-layer 3D flash memory, matching the technology of leading Korean manufactures.

CXMT is an IDM specialized in DRAM manufacturing. The company was founded in 2016 in Hefei, Anhui as a joint venture between Hefei municipal government and Beijing-based GigaDevice, a NOR flash memory design house. Building on the technology and patent portfolio acquired from Qimonda, a bankrupted German DRAM maker, CXMT developed 19-nanometer DRAM chips with its own R&D work. In September 2019, CXMT launched mass production of 8Gb DDR4 DRAM modules, China's first indigenously developed DRAM chip on par with international mainstream technology.

8.3.5 Semiconductor Equipment

While China has established a relatively complete semiconductor supply chain over the last three decades, the capital equipment industry has been largely neglected. Part of the reasons is a relatively small domestic market for equipment, and Chinese chipmakers have relied on imported machinery. In recent years, the National IC Fund has invested in a number of equipment makers in the Fund's first phase, and it is planning to target semiconductor equipment sector for massive funding in the second phase. A small number of Chinese semiconductor equipment makers have emerged, though they are not yet to compete with international leaders such as Applied Materials, ASML, or LAM Research.

NAURA Technology Group is China's largest semiconductor equipment maker with an annual sale of over 4 billion RMB (or 700 million USD) in 2019. NAURA was formed in 2017 by merging a group of state-owned semiconductor equipment makers in Beijing, a major capital equipment cluster in the pre-reform era. NAURA supplies oxidation/diffusion furnace, a variety of etchers, and cleaning equipment in IC manufacturing to leading Chinese foundries such as YMTC, SMIC, and Huahong.

Advanced Micro-Fabrication Equipment Corporation (AMEC) is another major Chinese semiconductor equipment maker. Founded by a group of returnees from Applied Materials in Shanghai, 2004, the company's main business is supplying etchers and MOCVD machines, though a large share of its sales goes into LED and photovoltaic chip fabrication, since China is the world's largest producer of both LED and solar photovoltaic cells. Nevertheless, AMEC uses the revenue derived from LED and PV industries to invest heavily in R&D, and the company has developed advanced etching equipment for advanced 7-nanometer manufacturing process.

Lithography machine is a critical technology in IC fabrication. The Netherlands' ASML monopolizes the production of the world's most advanced lithography machines with EUV technology used for 7-nanometer process node and below. The most advanced Chinese lithography machine maker is Shanghai Micro Electronics Equipment Co. (SMEE), which supplies relatively backward 90-nanometer process machines. SMEE is expected to deliver 28-nanometer lithography in 2021, but its technology has not been widely tested yet because of SMEE's low volume.

8.3.6 Semiconductor Materials

To feed the growing demands of local foundries, China has invested heavily in semiconductor materials in recent years. A number of startup companies have emerged in this industry, and many existing chemical makers have diversified into supplying electronic specialty gases used in IC fabrication. The leading Chinese silicon wafer maker is Shanghai-based Zing Semiconductor Corporation (ZingSemi), founded in 2014 by Richard Ru-Gin Chang, the aforementioned SMIC founder. In 2018, ZingSemi launched the first domestically manufactured 12-inch silicon wafers, ending China's complete reliance on imported 12-inch wafers for IC fabrication. ZingSemi and a number of wafer makers and chemical suppliers were merged in 2015 to form National Silicon Industry Group (NSIG), currently the largest semiconductor material provider in China.

8.3.7 EDA Tools

Comparing to China's limited but expanding presence in semiconductor equipment and materials, the country's progress in developing a software industry to support IC design is even more limited. Internationally, the EDA tools market is dominated by three American companies: Synopsys, Cadence, and Mentor Graphics. Most Chinese design houses, including Huawei's HiSilicon, depends on EDA software from the three companies. The largest and most sophisticated Chinese EDA company is Beijing-based Huada Empyrean, which may be the only Chinese company that can offer toolsets covering the complete design flow for IC chips. Despite the fact that the size of Huada Empyrean is still tiny compared to the largest three vendors, the leading American firms have an advantage that Chinese firms cannot replicate in a short time: the leading EDA vendors have close relationships with foundries, from which they can participate in the development of new, advanced process nodes and maintain their leads in EDA software (Fuller 2021).

8.3.8 IP Cores

IP core is an area where China relies heavily on foreign technology. Among the world's top ten semiconductor IP providers, there is only one China Mainland company, VeriSilicon. The Shanghai-based VeriSilicon was founded in 2001 by a group of returnees from Silicon Valley. The company's main business is in providing image processing IPs, a lucrative market but hardly critical for China's ambition in technological independence.

Most Chinese semiconductor companies rely on IPs provided by the UK-based ARM (owned by Japan's Softbank), the world's largest semiconductor IP supplier, to design processor chips. This dependence creates a potential danger if ARM's IPs are under the U.S. government's export controls or if ARM is acquired by an American company (as Nvidia is currently in talks of acquiring ARM). One possible solution to reduce foreign dependence is to adopt the open-sourced CPU architecture, RISC-V, of which Chinese companies have been actively participating in the development.

8.4 Concluding Remarks

Through decades of investment and development, China has built an emerging semiconductor industry. As analysis in this Chapter shows, the Chinese semiconductor industry has established presence in all three main steps of IC manufacturing: design, fabrication, and packaging and testing. While not all Chinese semiconductor capabilities are cutting-edge or even mainstream, such a complete supply chain is still remarkable, especially given the fact that the U.S. has consistently limited the exports of advanced machinery to China. Nevertheless, there are significant weaknesses in China's semiconductor supply chain, especially in the supportive industries of capital equipment and software tools.

The U.S. government's recent chokepoint strategy has leveraged the American advantage and Chinese disadvantage in capital equipment and EDA tools. Such policies, if implemented through a major expansion of export controls on chips and equipment to China, will surely slow down China's technological development and weaken commercial competitiveness of Chinese companies. However, a relatively complete domestic semiconductor supply chain will provide sufficient resilience to Chinese companies for their short-term survival. The irony is, under the pressure of current U.S. policy, Chinese companies are more aligned to their government's goal of indigenous innovation than they were a decade ago. In the long run, Chinese companies and government would accelerate the development of de-Americanized technology.

That being said, China can find it challenging if it intends to dominate the global semiconductor industry in foreseeable future. While Chinese companies are more likely to benefit from the vast domestic market, as companies will source more chips, equipment, materials, and software from domestic suppliers, there are still significant obstacles for China to catch up in advanced semiconductor manufacturing. Certain technological leads enjoyed by today's leading players are simply too difficult to replace, whether that is TSMC's advanced foundry, or ASML's lithography machine, or American-made EDA tools. While China does benefit from a complete supply chain in the U.S.-China technology rivalry, China cannot and should not try to dominate the whole semiconductor industry.

In the next decade, while semiconductor technology will remain important, the winner in the U.S.-China technology rivalry might not be determined by the shrinking nodes of silicon-based transistors. The real opportunity and risk for both China and the U.S. could be lying on game-changing breakthroughs in quantum computing or third-generation semiconductors (also called wide band gap semiconductors). These new technologies and materials will induce architectural changes in information technology industries, obsoleting technological leads of incumbent players. In that regard, the real competition between the U.S. and China should be in science, not in trade policy.

References

Feng, K., & Li, Y. (2020). Employee Ownership and Industrial Innovation. *China Review, 20* (4), 39–68.

Fuller, D. B. (2016). *Paper Tigers, Hidden Dragons: Firms and the Political Economy of China's Technological Development.* Oxford University Press.

Fuller, D. (2021). China's Counter-Strategy to American Export Controls in Integrated Circuits. *China Leadership Monitor*, Issue No. 67 (Spring).

Hu, Q. (2006). *Road to Chips: Records from Ultra Large-Scale Integrated Circuit Project 909* (in Chinese). Beijing: Electronics Industry Press.

Lazonick, W., & Li, Y. (2013). *China's Path to Indigenous Innovation.* Working Paper.

Li, Y. (2016). State, Market, and Business Enterprise: Development of the Chinese Integrated Circuit Foundries. In Y. Zhou, W. Lazonick, & Y. Sun (Eds.), *China as an Innovation Nation* (pp. 306–332). Oxford, UK: Oxford University Press.

Li, Y. (2017). *Innovation Pathways in the Chinese Economy.* PhD Dissertation, Georgia Institute of Technology.

Mays, S. K. (2013). *Rapid Advance: High Technology in China in the Global Electronic Age.* PhD Dissertation, Columbia University.

Simon, D., & Rehn, D. (1987). Innovation in China's Semiconductor Components Industry: The Case of Shanghai. *Research Policy, 16*(5), 259–277.

State Council of the People's Republic of China. (2015). Made in China 2025 Technical Area Roadmap. (In Chinese), October 29, 2015. Retrieved from http://www.cae.cn/cae/html/files/2015-10/29/20151029105822561730637.pdf.

Xi, J. (2016). Talk at the Cyber Security and Information Work Forum. (In Chinese), April 19, 2016. Retrieved from http://jhsjk.people.cn/article/28303771.

Xi, J. (2020). Talk at Scientists' Forum. (In Chinese), September 11, 2020. Retrieved from http://jhsjk.people.cn/article/31858850.

CHAPTER 9

The New Chinese Dream: Perspectives, Potentials and Weaknesses

John R. McIntyre and Francesca Spigarelli

Abstract The concluding chapter provides historical and analytical perspectives on China's strengths and weaknesses in achieving the centennial goals which have driven the long path of Chinese economic history since its opening to the world economy. The chapter raises the fundamental question: have industrial policies worked? It reviews the question against the background of a fierce academic debate "over whether China should continue to exercise the industrial policies that undergirded its rise to prominence," as quoted scholars have noted. The chapter concludes on the emergence of a Chinese "third revolution" as a unique and differentiated policy model.

J. R. McIntyre (✉)
Georgia Tech CIBER, Scheller College of Business, Atlanta, GA, USA
e-mail: john.mcintyre@scheller.gatech.edu

F. Spigarelli
Department of Law, University of Macerata, Macerata, Italy
e-mail: Francesca.spigarelli@unimc.it

F. Spigarelli, J. R. McIntyre (eds.), *The New Chinese Dream*, Palgrave Studies of Internationalization in Emerging Markets,
https://doi.org/10.1007/978-3-030-69812-6_9

Keywords Industrial policies • Prospects of Chinese economy • Third revolution

9.1 Introduction

This specialized volume, *The New Chinese Dream: Industrial Transition in the Post-Pandemic Era*, has sought to focus on post-covid Chinese industrial and innovation policy as the country moves towards new objectives it has set for its 2049 centennial.

These goals not only will shape China's innovation potential but also posit to make China the premier global advanced manufacturing national economy. This volume adds to a rich and growing body of literature chronicling China's unexpected economic and sectoral booms of the past three decades (a recent exemplar is found in Brandt and Rawski 2019). It does so by focusing sharply on eight select industrial and innovatory sectors and cross-cutting questions.

Angus Maddison, the most notable economic historian of China's decline and rise as a global economic power, established that China was the world's largest economy in 1820 for an estimated, then, 32.9% of global GDP (2001). Internal strife, natural disasters, distortive economic policies, and foreign wars resulted in China's share of GDP falling to 5.2% by 1952 and by 1978 it had further fallen to 4.9% (Maddison 2001). It is against this historical background that China's industrial policy, as an emanation of government's and party's will and vision, must be understood. Today, China's GDP amounts to 15.5% of the world economy and when computing it on a purchasing power parity basis it is closer to 23%. Its annual GDP growth is expected at 5.8 percent in 2022, with a per capita GDP expected to continue growing reaching $10,839 U.S. dollars in 2020 (Statista 2020). While these statistics have been subjected to much criticism and claims that China's economy is far smaller than official data indicate, they are the statistics generally accepted (Wildau 2019).

The Chinese government, reflecting these numerical achievements, has set two centennial goals or *Liang ge yibai nian* targeting, first, year 2021 and then, second, year 2049, marking the centenaries of the Chinese Communist Party and the People's Republic of China respectively. As seen in Chap. 1, by 2021, the Chinese government aims 'to build a moderately prosperous society in all respects' with an emphasis on targeting poverty reduction and alleviation measures, doubling GDP and per capita income for both urban and rural residents. By 2049, the Chinese government's goal is far more ambitious and aims to 'build a modern socialist country that is prosperous, strong, democratic, culturally advanced and harmonious". It looks, to most observers, that China is well on the road to achieve the first goals. Uncertainties surround the path to the second centennial goal and are directly related to the ability to achieve its premier global manufacturing power status. Fulfilling these two centennial goals, incorporated into the Chinese Communist Party's constitution in 2012, will shape China's long-term economic plans and inform the country's approach to everything from geopolitical issues to climate change policies—and will ultimately underlie the CCP's legitimacy as China's governing party.

9.2 The Role of Industrial Policies in China

Such target-setting raises an obvious question. Have industrial policies, put in place for the past forty years, worked? Economic achievements aside, a ferocious academic debate has been raging "over whether China should continue to exercise the industrial policies that undergirded its rise to prominence" (Dollar et al. 2020, p. 259). The question of industrial policies has come back into the limelight of policy and academic debates globally since the financial crisis of 2008. Since at least Jean-Baptiste Colbert, France's finance minister under Louis XIV in the seventeenth century, governments have used taxes, tariffs, State ownership and public sector management, as well as outright subsidies to cultivate national champions. Government-led, dirigiste, industrial policies look attractive, all the more, if markets are highly imperfect, a common occurrence in developing countries in catch-up mode. This pattern fits to perfection the Chinese case, thus far.

The Trump administration in the US has criticized the Chinese government for using industrial policies as a form of "economic aggression," considering it violative of the World Trade Organization's rules, thereby hurting the US and other economies. Such charges have fueled a trade "war" between the two economic giants in which the role of government's industrial policies is at the heart of the raging controversies. Whether these skirmishes can be understood within the "Thucydides trap" framework laid out by Graham Allison remains to be seen (Allison 2017).

The US, in part with the Europeans, has responded by deploying the full array of tariff measures, export control laws, intellectual property safeguard mechanisms as well as strengthened visa issuance rules. Robert Lighthizer, U.S. Special Trade Representative, declared on June 15, 2018 that "China's government is aggressively working to undermine America's high-tech industries and our economic leadership through unfair trade practices and industrial policies like Made in China 2025" (Lighthizer 2018). There can no clearer expression of concern over China's long-term objective of becoming the leader among the world's manufacturing powers by 2049. China's leadership has responded to this looming protracted conflict with a new concept, that of "dual circulation." It centers on internal circulation, emphasizing paramount reliance on the domestic economy, supplemented by external circulation as necessary, and leaning heavily on ambitious industrial policy goals. This turning inward could be interpreted as import substitution as Chinese industry reaches higher levels of autonomy.

In conditions of global pandemic, the role of industrial and innovation policy takes on a different coloration. The pandemic and post-pandemic periods will most probably solidify self-reliance ambitions giving further impulsion to digital and technological sovereignty. Both the European Union and the United States in anticipation of industrial acquisitions of strategic assets in biotechnologies have tightened investment prior screening tools (Arcestati and Rasser 2020). The post-pandemic period, in the ideal, should not result in industrial isolationism and digital mistrust. Beijing's ambition to lead in AI, quantum computing, genomics, 5G through China's plan to boost indigenous innovation, through subsidies, and protectionism threatens market dynamics.

The use of industrial policy in China has generated other controversies. One is found in the role of heavy-handed state guidance of natural monopolies such as shipbuilding and electricity generation, textbook examples, resulting in over-capacity, undermining the sectors supposed to benefit from government largesse. Liu has cogently demonstrated that Chinese state support is most value-added when the recipients are industrial sectors manufacturing essential inputs for other upstream or downstream related sectors (Liu 2019). Another controversy, bearing on China's ambitious "Made in China 2025" (MIC 25) and 2049 centennial goals, relates to the proper path and speed of innovation and how the Chinese pattern and trajectory of growth should respond to China's new economic status. Breznitz and Murphree (2012) argued that the run of Chinese industrial development had made the country into the world's ultimate workshop but that it would be mistaken to compare such achievements to an idealized grand Silicon Valley. Thus, arguing that process innovation was more suited to the multiple obstacles faced by China's dual economy rather than leading-edge innovation.

"Made in China 2025," the national strategic plan, as analyzed in previous Chapters, quickly became a profound assertion of the Chinese state' s intent to shift China from a low-end manufacturer to become a high-end manufacturer powerhouse with targeted investment in research and development and a clear emphasis on "state of the art" innovation. Exemplars of targeted fields include, *inter alia*, information technology, aerospace, biotech, smart manufacturing, pharmaceuticals, robotics. It was further buttressed by a distinct set of new industrial goals to push for sector and region-specific policies, inclusive of Chinese mega-cluster cities, to attract investors and innovators.

"Made in China 2025," foundation stone for the 2049 goals, established nine foundational priorities which bear review: (1) improving manufacturing innovation, (2) integrating advanced technology into industrial process, (3) strengthening the core industrial base, (4) fostering Chinese brands, (5) enforcing green manufacturing, compatible with growth goals, (6) promoting breakthroughs in the ten key sectors identified, (7) modernizing the manufacturing sector's chains, (8) promoting service-oriented manufacturing and related service sectors, and (9) internationalizing manufacturing, within the confines of a changing global political economy. Each of these priorities evolved its own metrics as to progress realized, distance to cover, to reach 2049.

More recently and to the expressed alarm of many in the United States and the European Union, China has put in place a strategy of establishing its own *de jure* and *de facto* technical and operational standards, with an intermediate time goal of 2035. Standards are the ultimate form of power projection in industrial competitiveness (CSIS 2020). This new policy has the resulting effect of challenging extant technical and operational standards largely set heretofore in the European Union and, to a lesser extent, in the United States. China has indeed embarked on a new course which lights the road to 2049.

9.3 China's Four Main Challenges

Assessing where China's future growth path lays, Wang defined four major processes which China will face for the coming thirty years as it upgrades its industrial and innovatory capabilities (Dollar et al. 2020, pp. 259–279). These four challenges, reflected in all the select topics addressed in this volume, are occurring simultaneously, making China the only country facing such an overlap of rapid reforms impacting industrial policy issues.

Firstly, China faces the challenge, as per capita GDP increases, of shifting resource allocation from agriculture to manufacturing to service, a process under way, with societal and labor market implications. The role of "state of the art" innovation in this process is central as detailed in the volume's chapter by Enderwick.

Second, it faces the dilemma of most transitional economies, still undecided as to the speed of implementation, of moving from a centrally planned economy to a mixed market economy. Industrial and innovation policies have been one of the key reform instruments in China's economy since the late 1980's, playing a decisive role in moving the Chinese growth path from a command planned economy to a more "market economy with Chinese characteristics." This is squarely addressed in the chapter by Sanpaolo, Di Tommaso and Liack. The concrete quantitative goals of "Made in China 2025" is to reduce China's reliance on foreign technology while increasing the domestic market share for key Chinese products, creating a large and relatively self-sufficient domestic market. Industrial policy has thus become one of the principal pillars of the Chinese transition towards a modified economic system. It is worth recalling that industry contributes some forty percent to Chinese GDP, roughly twenty eight percent to employment figures. It is truly one of the proactive means to become an international leader in innovation and technology (World Bank 2019).

Third, since its entry into the World Trade Organization in 2001, China has become the largest exporting country in the world, deeply engaged in the process of economic globalization of its industrial base. This global economic integration of the Chinese economy may have led to an overdependence on exports. The issue is addressed head-on in the chapter by Herrala, with its attendant implications. This third process also saw the transformation of state-owned enterprises into multinational enterprises. It also entailed significant international technology transfer, with all the ensuing issues of adequate intellectual property protection and technological leads' erosion by China's trading partners, as well as a greater internal liberalization of capital but also the status of the renminbi as a global transactional and possibly reserve currency in Asia. Yet, one of the great paradoxes for today's China is its leadership's push to position the country as a champion of globalization in a post-Covid world while, at the same time, increasingly restrict the free flow of information, goods, and capital between China and the world at large. At stake, reaching the commanding heights of global advanced manufacturing and technology innovation and achieving a measure of strategic autarky. This third process and the related paradox are amply illustrated in several of the volume's expert chapters by authors Lepore and Chen (life sciences), McIntyre and Hoadley (commercial aircraft manufacturing), Yi (semiconductor industries), and Jolly (digital transformation technologies), among others.

Lastly, the ongoing process of China's rise as a global geopolitical actor is inextricably linked to its industrial and innovatory capabilities and mirrored in such initiatives as the Belt and Road Initiative and the Regional Comprehensive Economic Partnership of 2020. This theme is reflected in the piece by Papageorgiou and dos Santos Cardoso.

In conclusion, as Elisabeth Economy notes, in a well-received book, President Xi seeks a unique policy model known as the "third revolution". This model, following her analysis, tracks four dimensions: long game in historical time favoring control rather than competition; centralizing power and control over information; reclaiming China's greatness; and a challenge to reconcile an illiberal state seeking leadership in a liberal world order. We can only speculate that perhaps this growth model "might become a standard bearer for other countries disenchanted with the American and European models of liberal democracy" (Economy 2018, p. 12).

References

Allison, G. (2017). *Destined for War: Can America and China Escape Thucydides's Trap*. New York, NY: Mariner Book.

Arcestati, R., & Rasser, M. (2020, May 29). China's Post-Covid 19 'Techno-Nationlist' Industrial Policy. *EU Observer*. Retrieved from https://euobserver.com/opinion/148449.

Brandt, L., & Rawski, T. G. (Eds.). (2019). *Policy, Regulation, and Innovation in China's Electricity and Telecom Industries*. Cambridge: Cambridge University Press.

Breznitz, D., & Murphree, M. (2012). *Run of the Red Queen: Government, Innovation, Globalization, and Economic Growth in China*. New Haven, CT.

CSIS, Center for Strategic and International Studies, China Power. (2020, June 30). *China's Standard-Setting Agenda 2035: A Conversation with Emily de la Bruyère*. Washington, DC. China Standards 2035 Archives | ChinaPower Project (csis.org).

Dollar, D., Huang, Y., & Yao, Y. (Eds.). (2020). *China 2049: Economic Challenges of a Rising Global Power*. Washington, DC: Brookings Institution Press.

Economy, E. C. (2018). *The Third Revolution: Xi Jinping and the New Chinese State*. Oxford: Oxford University Press.

Lighthizer, R. (2018, June 15). USTR Issues Tariffs on Chinese Products in Response to Unfair Trade Practices. Retrieved from USTR Issues Tariffs on Chinese Products in Response to Unfair Trade Practices | United States Trade Representative.

Liu, E. (2019). Industrial Policies in Production Networks. *Quarterly Journal of Economics, 134*(4).

Maddison, A. (2001). *The World Economy: A Millenial Perspective*. Paris: OECD.

Statista. (2020). Retrieved from https://www.statista.com/statistics/270439/chinas-share-of-global-gross-domestic-product-gdp/#:~:text=China's%20share%20of%20global%20gross%20domestic%20product%20(GDP)%202009%2D2025&text=The%20graph%20shows%20China's%20share,share%20was%20about%2017.39%20percent.

Wildau, G. (2019, March 6). China's Economy is 12% Smaller than Official Data say, Study Finds. *Financial Times*.

World Bank and Development Research Center of the State Council. (2019). *Innovative China: New Drivers of Growth*. Washington, DC: IBDR, World Bank Group.

Index

F. Spigarelli, J. R. McIntyre (eds.), *The New Chinese Dream*, Palgrave Studies of Internationalization in Emerging Markets, https://doi.org/10.1007/978-3-030-69812-6